In Search of Chaco

The publication of this book was made possible by generous gifts from
Maggie and Christian Andersson for the Loretto Chapel of Santa Fe,
William S. Cowles, and the Ethel-Jane Westfeldt Bunting Foundation.

Aerial photgraph of Pueblo Bonito made by Charles Lindbergh in 1929.

In Search of Chaco

New Approaches
to an Archaeological Enigma

Edited by David Grant Noble

A School of American Research
Popular Southwestern Archaeology Book

School of American Research Press
Santa Fe, New Mexico

School of American Research Press
Post Office Box 2188
Santa Fe, New Mexico 87504-2188
www.sarweb.org

Director: James F. Brooks
Executive Editor: Catherine Cocks
Copy Editor: Jane Kepp
Designer: Katrina Lasko
Maps: Molly O'Halloran
Production Manager: Cynthia Dyer
Proofreader: Margaret J. Goldstein
Indexer: Catherine Fox
Printed and bound by C & C Offset Printing Co., LTD.

Library of Congress Cataloging-in-Publication Data

In Search of Chaco : New Approaches to an Archaeological Enigma / edited by David Grant Noble.
p. cm.
Updated ed. of: New light on Chaco Canyon. 1st ed. c1984.
"A School of American Research popular southwestern archaeology book."
Includes bibliographical references and index.
ISBN 1-930618-42-5 (pa : alk. paper) — ISBN 1-930618-54-9 (cl : alk. paper)
1. Pueblo Indians—Antiquities. 2. Indians of North America—New Mexico—Chaco Canyon Region—Antiquities.
3. Chaco Canyon Region (N.M.)—Antiquities. 4. New Mexico—Antiquities.
I. Noble, David Grant. II. New light on Chaco Canyon.
E99.P9I5 2004
978.9'82--dc22
2004005447

Cover photograph (front): Hungo Pavi ruins looking toward Fajada Butte, David Grant Noble
Cover photograph (back): Interior walls, Pueblo Bonito, George H. H. Huey

Contents

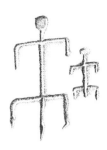

Illustrations

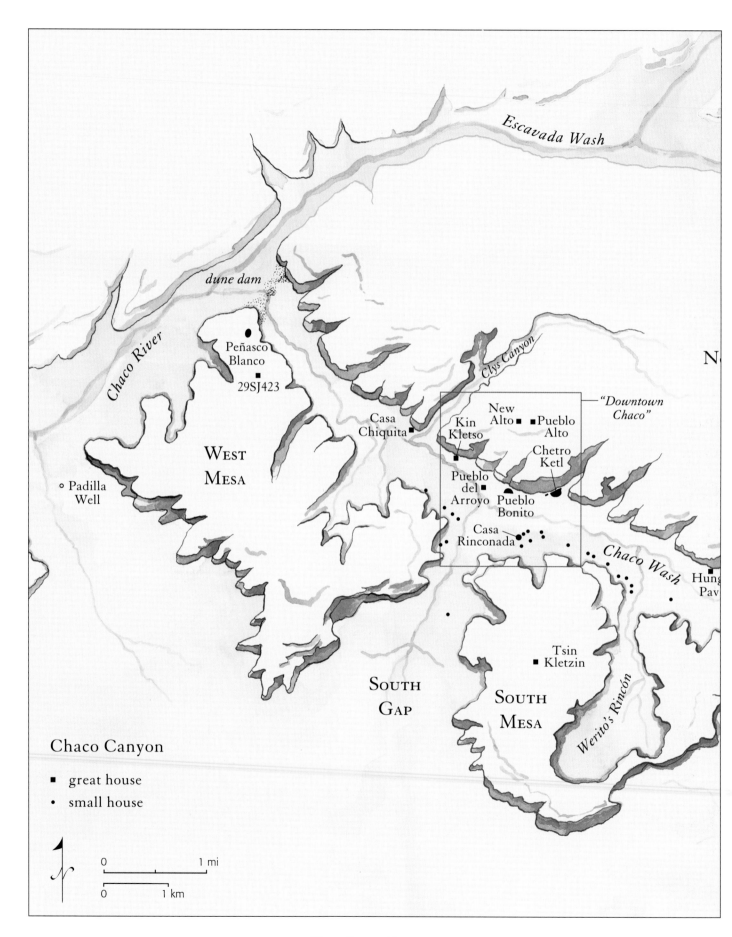

Escavada Wash

dune dam

Chaco River

Peñasco
Blanco

29SJ423

Clys Canyon

WEST
MESA

Casa
Chiquita

New
Alto ■ ■ Pueblo
Alto

"Downtown
Chaco"

N

Kin
Kletso

Chetro
Ketl

Padilla
Well

Pueblo
del
Arroyo

Pueblo
Bonito

Casa
Rinconada

Chaco Wash

Hung
Pav

SOUTH
GAP

SOUTH
MESA

Tsin
Kletzin

Werito's Rincón

Chaco Canyon

■ great house

• small house

N

0 _____ 1 mi

0 _____ 1 km

x   Chaco Canyon Map

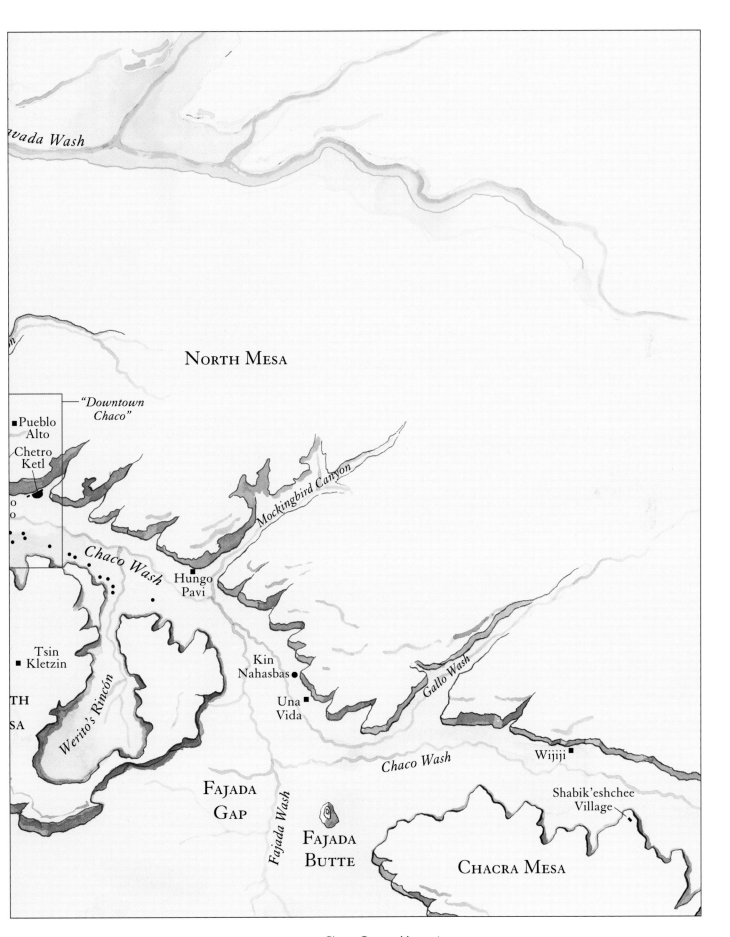

Wada Wash

NORTH MESA

"*Downtown Chaco*"

■ Pueblo Alto

Chetro Ketl

Mockingbird Canyon

Chaco Wash

■ Hungo Pavi

Tsin Kletzin ■

NTH SA

Werito's Rincón

Kin Nahasbas ●

Una Vida ■

Gallo Wash

Wijiji ■

Chaco Wash

FAJADA GAP

Fajada Wash

FAJADA BUTTE

Shabik'eshchee Village ◆

CHACRA MESA

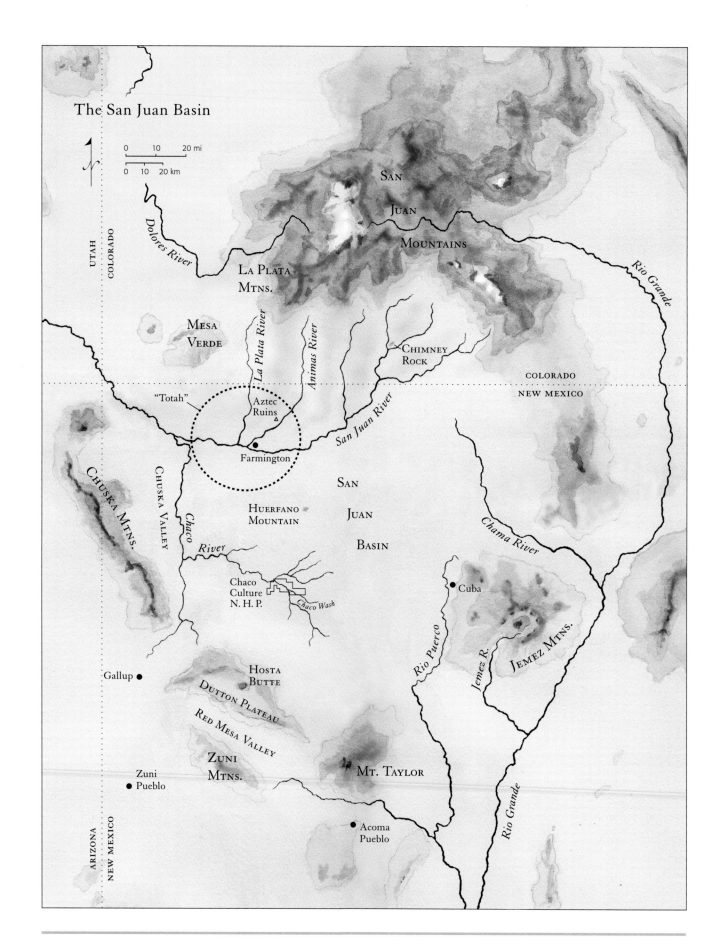

The San Juan Basin

0   10   20 mi
0   10   20 km

UTAH
COLORADO

Dolores River

SAN

JUAN

MOUNTAINS

Rio Grande

LA PLATA
MTNS.

MESA
VERDE

La Plata River

Animas River

CHIMNEY
ROCK

COLORADO
NEW MEXICO

"Totah"

Aztec
Ruins △

Farmington

SAN

JUAN

BASIN

CHUSKA MTNS.

CHUSKA VALLEY

Chaco

River

Huerfano
Mountain

Chama River

Cuba

Chaco
Culture
N.H.P.

Chaco Wash

Rio Puerco

Jemez R.

JEMEZ MTNS.

Gallup ●

HOSTA
BUTTE

DUTTON PLATEAU

RED MESA VALLEY

ZUNI
MTNS.

MT. TAYLOR

Zuni
● Pueblo

ARIZONA
NEW MEXICO

● Acoma
Pueblo

Rio Grande

Preface

David Grant Noble

When I first visited Chaco Canyon with a friend nearly fifty years ago, I had no idea that the place was more than just a canyon in the desert. We were easterners, exploring the Southwest for the first time. It was a late August afternoon, we had been driving all day, and we were looking for a place to camp off the highway. The road to the canyon was a good deal rougher then than it is now, and in places we had to detour around washouts by driving across the desert terrain—an interesting exercise in a Volkswagen Beetle. As we neared Chaco, we noted ominous clouds dragging dark streaks of rain across the bleak expanses of the San Juan Basin and wondered how the road would be ahead.

Finally we entered the canyon and turned into a pull-off along the road. As we got out of the car to stretch our legs, we noticed the crumbling remains of a large building—some kind of western ghost town, we assumed—and wandered over. The architecture was unfamiliar: exquisite masonry, empty spacious rooms, and curious circular chambers sunk into the ground. We didn't know what we were looking at, nor could we find anyone to ask. Perhaps that is the best way to see Pueblo Bonito for the first time.

David Noble

That night I slept under a ledge near the campground, awakened from time to time by the spectacle of light and sound emanating from distant storms. In the morning, a park ranger enlightened us about what we had seen the previous day. Chaco Canyon and Pueblo Bonito made a lasting impression on both of us, and it became clear to me that my years of schooling in the East had omitted a notable chapter in American history.

The late archaeologist Cynthia Irwin Williams, who excavated Salmon Ruins, not far north of Chaco Canyon, coined the term "Chaco phenomenon" in a paper she delivered at the 1975 Pecos Conference. It fast became part of the Chacoan vocabulary. Professionals used it, popular writers liked it, and it even became the title of a traveling museum exhibition. Chaco certainly was phenomenal; in the American Southwest there was nothing else like it. Its culture emerged in the late 800s CE ("of the common era," the equivalent of AD), reached a climax between about 1035 and 1135, and was in decline—in Chaco Canyon, at least—by 1140. The Chaco phenomenon lasted more than two and a half centuries. That's five lifetimes, ten generations, and longer than the United States has been a nation.

Still, why a "phenomenon"? The monumentality and fine workmanship of the Chacoans' architecture have much to do with it. And the "great houses" of the central canyon (to use another coined term), with their roadways and built landscape, have an urban look. "Downtown Chaco," in fact, is another addition to the scholarly vernacular. In the past thirty years, as researchers have discovered how widely great-house building extended beyond the canyon, they have come to recognize that the phenomenon was a system of some kind—far-reaching, interconnected, and seemingly encompassing common beliefs. How that system worked is difficult to reconstruct archaeologically or prove scientifically, but it certainly existed and had its own rules and patterns. With its outstanding architecture, linear roads, built landscape, cultural interconnectedness, and longevity, Chaco was and remains an amazing phenomenon.

When I put together the book *New Light on Chaco Canyon* (SAR Press, 1984) twenty-five years after my first visit to Chaco, I was motivated partly by a desire to fill the hole in my own education and, I assumed, that of many others. I also had become aware of a vital and growing general interest in the Southwest's Native American culture. Americans' desire to better understand their multifaceted heritage continues to expand. Archaeologists, and especially a dedicated group of Southwestern researchers, can be passionate about the subject. Some have devoted the major part of their professional lives—more than twenty-five years in some cases—to investigating and pondering Chaco Canyon. I'd call that passion.

In my view, these people who study Chaco year after year—in the field, in the laboratory, in the library, at conferences, and in Native communities—are themselves a sort of phenomenon. They certainly have stick-to-itiveness, even when solutions to the Chacoan "mystery" seem out of reach. The contributors to this volume fit the profile, but they are only part of a larger field of scholars doing everything from plotting the astronomical alignments of great houses to creating a Chaco digital archive. Since the days of William Henry Jackson, Victor Mindeleff, and Richard Wetherill, the scholars and diggers who have tried to throw light on Chacoan culture are legion. Just to create a complete bibliography of their efforts is a daunting task, but James Judge is presently undertaking to do exactly that.

The contributors to this volume may be among the front-runners of Chacoan research today, but they recognize that future generations will regard them as just a phase in the ever-unfolding process of discovery. This, too, is part of the Chaco phenomenon, which includes the Chacoans themselves, the scholars and writers, the artists, photographers, and musicians, the preservationists, the tourists, the modern pilgrims, and even the readers of these pages. Chaco is a place, a past, and a process.

One might ask, Why this book at this time? As some contributors point out, little basic research—in archaeology, that usually means digging—has taken place in the past twenty years. What has happened has been less a product of shovel and trowel than of the mind: analysis, comparison, interpretation, discussion, and debate. New questions are being asked and old ones reviewed. Where did the great-house idea originate and how were these buildings used? What are the implications of a recently discovered prehistoric natural dam spanning Chaco Wash? How did these ancient people organize themselves, their space, their time, their world? Were they violent or peaceable? What, really, were the so-called roads? How does Chaco compare with other archaeological sites in the world? Did Chaco end in the 1100s or carry on in some fashion? Who were the people of Chaco Canyon and who are their descendants? These are some of the issues addressed in the following pages.

Since my first visit to Pueblo Bonito in 1959, I have managed to fill out that gap in my education to some extent. As I have learned more about the Chacoans and their remarkable accomplishments, the canyon has acquired new meanings for me and posed questions I could not have imagined as a twenty-year-old. At the same time, the empty rooms and sunken kivas still reveal few clues to the history they have witnessed. The unknown still far outweighs the known. In that sense, perhaps Chaco is a metaphor for our search for knowledge—the closer we get to it, the more elusive it becomes.

Acknowledgments

A portion of Pueblo Bonito at sunset.

The pleasant task of bringing this book together was a cooperative one. I especially want to thank the writers for sharing their knowledge and expertise, providing illustrations, and offering good counsel. For their support, I also thank Russ Bodnar, G. B. Cornucopia, Dabney Ford, and Lewis Murphy of Chaco Culture National Historical Park; Stephen and Kathy Durand; Inara Edrington of the National Park Service's Western Archaeological and Conservation Center; Richard Friedman; Jane Kepp of Kepp Editorial; Marcia Logsdon for the use of her late husband's aerial photographs; Terry Morgart of the Hopi Cultural Preservation Office; Michael Piscopo of the Malta Tourist Office; Joyce Raab of the Chaco Archive at the University of New Mexico; and John Stein of the Navajo Nation Historic Preservation Department. Patricia McCreery deserves special acknowledgment for contributing her fine drawings of petroglyphs and architecture. Finally, my thanks go to the School of American Research for facilitating work on this book by providing me with a 2003 summer scholarship.

A Chaco Canyon Chronology

BCE (before the common era)

Paleo-Indian hunter-gatherers in region.

Archaic people hunting and foraging in region.

CE (of the common era)

First sedentary population in canyon. Basketmaker III people living in pithouse communities such as Shabik'eshchee Village.

Ancestral Pueblo people living in pithouses and starting to build small, aboveground pueblos.

850   Initial construction begins on Pueblo Bonito, Peñasco Blanco, and Una Vida. Continued use of pithouses to late 900s. Population growth. Active turquoise and pottery trade.

1035–1080   Major great-house construction period. Population decrease in mid-1000s.

Chaco system at its peak.

Early 1100s   Drought, collapse of regional outlier system, depopulation of Chaco Canyon. Building boom at Aztec West and Aztec East.

Temporary repopulation of Chaco Canyon.

First archaeological evidence of Navajos living in Chaco area.

1800s   Visits by Spanish and American military and survey expeditions.

Navajos removed to Fort Sumner by US military under Kit Carson. Return to homeland in 1868.

Wetherill homestead established at Pueblo Bonito. Hyde Exploring Expedition begins excavations in Pueblo Bonito.

1907   Chaco Canyon becomes a national monument.

In Search of Chaco

Figure 1.1. Hungo Pavi, looking toward Fajada Butte.

Chaco's *one* Golden Century

W. James Judge

In the hundred years between 1030 and 1130 CE, residents of the central San Juan Basin of northwestern New Mexico expended almost unbelievable human energy to create a cultural landscape of epic proportions, a truly enduring architectural masterpiece. They constructed massive buildings, great kivas, formal stairways up cliffs and mesas, a system of roads, and complex irrigation systems. Then, shortly after 1130, this unprecedented burst of human endeavor faded away almost as quickly as it had begun. These hundred years were Chaco Canyon's golden century, a period virtually unmatched elsewhere in the pre-Columbian Southwest.

Chaco Canyon is a desolate place by modern standards, seemingly devoid of most of the basic resources necessary to build the complex society that emerged there—which makes that accomplishment even more perplexing. Equally astounding is the rapidity with which the events took place. In 1030, only three structures were prominent on the Chaco Canyon landscape. Seventy years later, the canyon was home to a dozen massive buildings ("great houses"), each with hundreds of rooms. It boasted two separate great kivas, an extensive canal irrigation system, and a network of formal roads, ramps, and stairways connecting the great houses. Further, Chaco Canyon served as a ceremonial center linking possibly two hundred outlying sites dispersed throughout the San Juan Basin.

Archaeologists and visitors alike crave an explanation of the Chaco phenomenon. One way to attempt to explain it is to ask a series of questions that commonly come to mind when people visit Chaco Canyon and examine its archaeology.

Why Did Complexity Emerge in Chaco Canyon and Not Elsewhere?

An unusual configuration of environmental features made Chaco Canyon a rarity in the San Juan Basin. Reconstructions of the ancient climate, based on analyses of tree-ring patterns, fossil pollen, and the contents of packrat middens, indicate that the central San Juan Basin has been dry—with an average of 8.5 inches of annual precipitation—for several thousand years. Yet within the basin, Chaco Canyon is a geological anomaly. It runs generally east-west, exposing a set of cliffs in the bedrock sandstone several hundred feet high. The cliffs are especially pronounced on the north side of the canyon, where they are capped with an expanse of bare slickrock.

A series of side canyons, or *rincones* ("rincons" in English usage), channel runoff to the main canyon floor. The bottoms of the rincons and the canyon itself are level and thus were suitable for irrigation farming by the Chacoan people.

Another factor is that the canyon lies just west of Chacra Mesa, the highest mesa in the central San Juan Basin and an area rich in plants and animals that people could efficiently exploit. At its western edge, the canyon joins Escavada Wash, where the water table surfaces to provide even greater agricultural potential. Concentrated at the center of this near desert, then, Chaco Canyon's unique diversity of geological and biological resources made it a relative oasis in which a complex society had an opportunity to emerge.

Figure 1.2. Chaco Canyon from the air, looking northwest, with Fajada Butte in the foreground.

Why Did Chaco Flourish in the Eleventh Century and Not Earlier?

In the eleventh century, an increase in population and a combination of environmental factors converged to create, for the first time, the conditions necessary for Chaco Canyon's florescence. First, population had been gradually increasing in the central San Juan Basin since the advent of agriculture and village life in the sixth and seventh centuries. In the 900s CE, it was augmented by immigrants from the San Juan River region, over one hundred miles to the north. By the early 1000s, many large Pueblo settlements were dispersed throughout the basin, providing a population threshold for the emergence of complexity.

Second, the recent discovery of a former natural sand-dune dam just above the confluence of the Chaco and Escavada Washes suggests that sufficient water may have been impounded to create a marsh-like wetland at the west end of Chaco Canyon (see chapter 2). Together with an aggrading streambed, the dam would have raised the water table in the canyon sufficiently to increase the agricultural potential there even more.

The years from 990 to 1030 CE were ones of generally favorable precipitation. In the late 900s, taking advantage of the relatively bountiful environment and perhaps in order to store surplus farm produce, Chaco's inhabitants erected the canyon's first three great houses: Peñasco Blanco, Pueblo Bonito, and Una Vida. In addition, it is possible that canyon residents developed irrigation canals and gridded fields in the early 1000s to capture slickrock runoff during intense summer storms. Of the twenty-eight rincons adjoining the canyon, seventeen are known to have had irrigation systems, making Chaco one of the few places in North America in which people constructed extensive canal irrigation networks based solely on precipitation runoff. Thus, a combination of early-eleventh-century environmental factors and a general population increase set the stage for the emergence of the complex sociopolitical system that was to define Chaco's florescence.

Figure 1.3. Chetro Ketl, with the great kiva in the foreground.

What Happened in the Canyon to Create the Chaco Phenomenon?

Scholars have referred to the extraordinary developments that took place in Chaco Canyon as the "Chaco phenomenon." Archaeologists calculate that during the eleventh century, massive amounts of human energy—more than four hundred thousand person hours—were invested in construction in the canyon. The Chacoans built four new great houses—Hungo Pavi, Chetro Ketl, Pueblo Alto, and Pueblo del Arroyo—each according to a similar "D-shaped" architectural plan. They constructed two stand-alone great kivas, now known as Casa Rinconada and Kin Nahasbas, as well as several great kivas inside the plazas of existing structures. They engineered roads that connected the canyon great houses, and in some places they built dirt and masonry ramps and formal staircases to ascend the cliffs.

Chacoan researchers debate the motivating force behind this labor investment. Some have suggested that a ritual "sodality" emerged to integrate the diverse groups living within the canyon and its sur-

rounding areas. Sodalities are sociopolitical entities that draw their membership from kin-based organizations such as lineages and clans but are not themselves based on kinship. As such, they cut across existing social units and bind together diverse elements of a society. Perhaps a common belief system, manifested in shared rituals, helped the Chacoans cope with their challenging environment and inspired them to build ceremonial centers, just as other people around the world have built temples, cathedrals, and mosques. It might also have served to offset potential conflict among diverse cultural groups in the San Juan Basin. The leaders of this society might have been priests who controlled the organization through their knowledge of religious rituals.

Other scholars think that one or more formal sociopolitical entities called chiefdoms evolved in Chaco, with leadership based more on social rank or status than on ritual knowledge. In such chiefdoms, the power base of the leaders, or chiefs, can be seen in the accumulation of material wealth. This wealth can be envied and challenged and leads to increased competition both within and among chiefdoms. Archaeologists question this model of Chacoan complexity, noting that except at Pueblo Bonito, little evidence of such wealth has been uncovered in the excavated Chacoan great houses. Further, a political system that fostered competition among aspiring leaders would have been generally less capable of integrating the dispersed and diverse communities of the San Juan Basin. Religious authority, on the other hand, encompasses an entire belief system and so is more inclusive and integrative. Virtually all researchers recognize a strong ritual component to Chacoan authority and view the Chacoans as having formed a regional center with a compelling and integrating body of ceremony at its core.

Why Were the Chacoan Great Houses Built, and What Were They Used For?

The function of the Chacoan great houses has long puzzled researchers. Of the hundreds of small sites excavated by archaeologists in the Southwestern United States, most are clearly residential. They contain fire pits, storage and sleeping areas, and places to do household work. Chacoan great houses have few such features and few artifacts. As a result, archaeolo-

gists are now rethinking earlier interpretations in which they viewed great houses as residences for large numbers of people. Previous population estimates of more than ten thousand for Chaco Canyon are being reduced to fewer than two thousand. This revised view suggests that the great houses might not have been primarily residences. But if they were not, and if they did not house a large population, why were they built?

One clue might be found in the manner in which great houses were designed and constructed over time. As Chaco Canyon was emerging as a ceremonial center, perhaps the great houses were planned as monumental architectural expressions of Chacoan ritual. For example, Chetro Ketl, the largest of the D-shaped structures in the canyon, with three stories and some five hundred rooms, was built in distinct stages over an eighty- to ninety-year period in the eleventh century. Without written records, how did its builders adhere to its original architectural design throughout decades of construction? Perhaps the foundation for the entire structure was laid at the outset as a kind of master plan to guide the generations of workers who followed. The width of the foundation could have served to project the number

Figure 1.4. Reconstruction of Chetro Ketl by Robert Coffin, about 1930.

of stories to be constructed in later building stages. The maze of rooms found in the depths of such massive sites may have changed function as the building rose, ultimately serving as a structural support for the entire building. In this view, Chaco was at once a ceremonial center and a place of ritual architecture—a dramatic stage, as it were, for all to see and appreciate.

How Did the Chaco System Function during the Golden Century?

In the latter part of the eleventh century, Chaco Canyon reached the peak of its development as the architectural and ceremonial center of the San Juan Basin. Rainfall was generally above average from 1050 to 1080 CE, and the runoff irrigation system was probably producing sufficient crops to feed both residents and visitors to the canyon. During this time, residents of the San Juan Basin traveled to Chaco periodically to conduct ceremonies and to confirm their allegiance to the ritual system that served them well in their outlying settlements. A small group of priests may have resided in each canyon great house, which might also have housed pilgrims and served as storage places for ritual paraphernalia.

Particular groups living outside the canyon might have supplied the workforce to construct certain great houses there. Workers engaged in such construction, as well as in the building of great kivas and other public works, might have been housed in the small pueblos on the south side of the canyon, where the resident farmers lived. When their construction services were no longer needed, workers would have returned to their permanent settlements outside the canyon. Those making pilgrimages into the canyon might have contributed specific ceremonies to the mix and been supplied with seed corn or other useful goods for their return. The permanent canyon population, then, might have consisted of relatively few priests with authority over ceremonies and a limited number of farmers and maintenance workers. Of course, this population must have swelled during pilgrimage times and major construction episodes.

Constituents of the Chacoan ritual system living in the greater San Juan Basin and beyond probably came from varied cultural backgrounds and spoke different languages. Certainly, diverse peoples had lived there earlier, in Archaic and Basketmaker times. This diversity might have been reflected in the ownership of great houses and control of traditional ceremonies in the canyon. Again, the encompassing ritual that emerged in the early eleventh century might have integrated such factions and helped keep the peace. The same integrative capability might also have reinforced economic networks designed to redistribute the scarce and unequal resources of the San Juan Basin.

How Big Was the Chacoan System?

As many as two hundred great-house communities in the San Juan Basin display Chacoan characteristics, though they vary considerably in size, dates of occupation, and architecture. Not all have great kivas, and only a small number have formal roads nearby. Consequently, the size of the system integrated by Chacoan ritual at any given time is difficult to determine. Estimates range from thirty thousand to forty thousand square miles—an area about the size of Portugal. As primary components of the Chacoan system, outlying great houses might themselves have served as ritual centers for their surrounding Pueblo settlements. Persons of authority who lived in them might have organized periodic labor excursions and religious pilgrimages to Chaco Canyon, contributing to construction and ceremony there and confirming their affiliation with the larger ritual alliance.

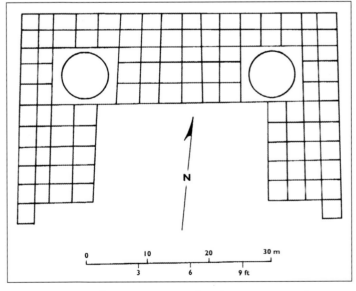

Figure 1.5. Plan of Wijiji, constructed in the 1100s. Note the small, compact rooms typical of late Chacoan great houses.

Figure 1.6. Typical desert terrain of the central San Juan Basin.

Why Did It Collapse in the Early Twelfth Century?

Because they depended on cultivating crops in an arid land, the Chacoans likely focused much of their ceremonialism on appeals for moisture. During the very late 1000s, a downturn in precipitation in the San Juan Basin must have contributed to major changes in the Chacoan system and stimulated ordinary Chacoans to seriously question the efficacy of the rituals being performed by their priests. Further, increasingly large influxes of visitors, drawn to the canyon on pilgrimages or work details, might have taxed the area's fragile environment to its limit. Perhaps in the Chaco phenomenon's successes were sown the seeds of its demise. Around 1100, the leadership may have decided to relocate the ceremonial center north to sites along the San Juan River and its tributaries, where the great houses of Salmon and Aztec were already under construction.

Following this shift, the early years of the twelfth century saw a definite improvement in the climate. This may have been the reason for new construction in the canyon, which by then had become ancillary to the new Aztec-Salmon center. Those left in Chaco constructed new great houses such as Kin Kletso and Wijiji in a different architectural style, resembling structures to the north in the Mesa Verde area. Unlike the earlier canyon great houses, these were erected in single building seasons. They also have a more residential than ritual appearance and may have been the homes of those who chose to remain in the once great ceremonial center. Regardless, the climate again turned bad after 1130, this time initiating one of the most severe and enduring Southwestern droughts on record—almost fifty years of below-average precipitation. As the twelfth century progressed, many great-house occupants, including those in Chaco Canyon, moved away from their homes.

In retrospect, one might regard the extraordinary construction in Chaco Canyon as a noble experiment in the adaptive potential of human society. Considering the canyon's relatively bountiful environment, it is understandable that it became the economic, social, and ritual center for the people of the San Juan Basin. Given the harsh environment of the basin as a whole and the diversity of its people and customs, one might expect social tensions and conflict to have arisen among disparate groups, and probably they did. Hallmarks of Chacoan expression, the elaborate social system and religious rituals that emerged would have served to integrate the people and contain such conflict. The extraordinary accomplishments that resulted endure today as central facets of the modern Pueblo world.

W. James Judge headed the National Park Service's Chaco Project from 1977 to 1985 and was coeditor of *Chaco and Hohokam: Prehistoric Regional Systems in the American Southwest.* His current interests include the electronic publication of archaeological research materials. He is an emeritus professor of anthropology at Fort Lewis College in Durango, Colorado.

Puebloan Farmers of the Chacoan World

two

R. Gwinn Vivian

On May 15, 1877, William Henry Jackson, pioneer photographer of the American West, discovered an ancient stairway behind Pueblo Bonito that allowed him to reach the cliff top for a spectacular view of the great house on his last day in Chaco Canyon. He had spent a week recording the major ruins in remarkable detail while camping in Chaco Wash beside "a few shallow pools of thick, pasty water." He ruefully commented that "the most important result . . . of this last discovery [the stairway] was the finding of a series of water pockets" containing "thousands of gallons of clear, cool, sweet water, a thing we had not seen for many days." The archaeologist Edgar Hewett once remarked that simply to get to Chaco Canyon, "the desert barrier must be crossed." Jackson's first attempt to reach Chaco from Fort Defiance had been thwarted because the Navajos "dread to visit it at this time of year on account of the well-known dearth of water."

But that desert barrier was penetrated many times in the past, beginning with nomadic Archaic gathering and hunting groups. They were followed by the first ancestral Pueblo Indians, who not only survived in Chaco Canyon but thrived. By combining a knowledge of the land and the weather with human ingenuity, the early Chacoans adapted successfully to their new homeland, at least for a time.

This homeland—the Chacoan world—encompasses almost ten thousand square miles of the northwest corner of New Mexico, a physiographic region of the Colorado Plateau known as the San Juan Basin. Mountain ranges whose names reflect the Pueblo, Spanish, and Navajo heritages of past explorers and residents surround the lower-lying interior land. The inner basin is marked by one major topographic feature, Chacra Mesa, through which Chaco Canyon was cut in several stages beginning about three hundred thousand years ago (see map, p. x-xi).

The combination of the uplifted mesa and the channeling canyon created an oasis of sorts in an otherwise semiarid and almost featureless land. Rising as high as six hundred feet above the south side of the canyon, Chacra Mesa supports life zones not found on the valley floor. Slight differences in precipitation and temperature permit the growth of piñon, juniper, and other higher-elevation plants that provided humans with useful medicines and foods, including piñon nuts, along with habitat for more upland-dwelling animals such as mule deer.

Farming in Chaco Canyon

The broad, flat canyon bottom was more suitable for farming. The runoff it received from the east, north, and south made it one of the best-watered places in the inner basin. The major drainage, Chaco Wash, runs from east to west through the canyon, receiving additional discharge from two intersecting valleys on the south and from multiple short side canyons, or rincons, on the north.

All this runoff comes from rain or melting snow. The amount of moisture entering the inner San Juan Basin and Chaco Canyon is conditioned to a large degree by the mountains surrounding the basin. These ranges form barriers to incoming storms and create a classic rain shadow effect. Continental atmospheric circulation systems, or "storm paths," also affect the quantity and timing of winter and

Figure 2.1. Chaco Wash with Fajada Butte in the distance.

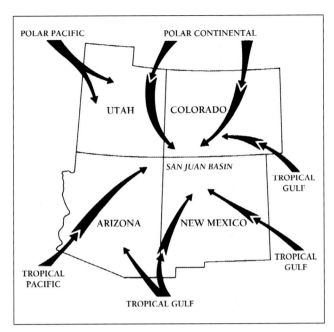

Figure 2.2. Storm paths that affect precipitation in the San Juan Basin.

summer precipitation in the basin. Southwestern Colorado lies near the southern limit of the snow-bearing winter path, and northwestern New Mexico sits on the northern edge of the summer rainfall path. This marginal positioning produces seasonal north-south differences within the basin and annual moisture differences if winter and summer storm paths shift slightly to the north or south. The ultimate effects of topographic and atmospheric factors on basin climate are highly variable rainfall and snowfall and an average annual precipitation of only 8.5 inches for Chaco Canyon.

The same factors influence temperature, which, with precipitation, is the most critical element for farmers. Seasonal temperature variations in the basin are extreme. Summers are hot, and winters can be cold to very cold. Record temperatures in Chaco Canyon have ranged from a high of 106 degrees F to a low of -38 degrees F. Corn usually is not damaged until temperatures drop below 30 degrees F, a "killing frost," but the plant does require between 110 and 130 days for full maturation. William Gillespie has noted that frost-free periods in valley bottoms such as Chaco Canyon are usually briefer than they are in uplands, shortening the growing season by thirty to thirty-five days. Fewer than half the years between 1960 and 1982 in Chaco Canyon

had 100 frost-free days, and no year had as many as 150. As Gillespie observed, "it is hard to believe anyone would ever try to farm there."

I have spent much of my career searching for the reasons Puebloan farmers first came to Chaco Canyon and, more importantly, the reasons they stayed there for more than six hundred years. The first residents actually were not farmers but Archaic gathering and hunting people who took seasonal advantage of the plants and animals on Chacra Mesa, a few seeps and springs in canyon alcoves, and the winter protection of rock shelters. The same amenities were attractive to the earliest farmers or part-time farmers who pushed into the canyon by at least 500 CE, lured by its runoff and adequate soils.

Recently, I had the good fortune to be involved in research that showed that the potential for farming in Chaco Canyon might have been enhanced for a while by an unusual geomorphic development that put cycles of arroyo cutting and filling in the canyon out of sync with regional channel dynamics. A natural sand dune formed at the western end of Chaco Canyon, near the great house called Peñasco Blanco, temporarily damming flood-waters flowing down the canyon and creating a broad, shallow lake. This dam effectively curtailed arroyo cutting in the canyon when such channeling started in the rest of the region in the mid-eighth century. Around 900 CE, the dune dam was breached, prompting a new cycle of arroyo cutting that lowered water tables and had other damaging consequences for Chacoan farmers.

Given the erraticism of Colorado Plateau climate, no ancestral Puebloan could have depended upon just one farming method. Seasonal, annual, and spatial changes in moisture, cycles of erosion and filling, and fluctuating groundwater levels all forced Puebloan people to use multiple techniques and social means to reduce the risk of running out of food. Chacoans, like other ancestral Puebloans, chose field locations that optimized yields and reduced the chances of crop failure. Within the canyon, good soils and exposure to the sun were important, but water remained the critical factor when they selected places to farm. Annual moisture was insufficient for dry farming under most conditions, so farmers planted crops where they would

Figure 2.3. The remains of a prehistoric natural sand-dune dam across the mouth of Chaco Wash are still visible today.

receive storm runoff or where they could be watered with captured runoff distributed through canals.

Runoff entering the canyon from the east, north, and south takes quite different patterns. Chaco Wash flows west through the canyon, carrying enormous quantities of water from many tributaries. When the wash is not entrenched, this water can spread thinly over much of the canyon bottom, including fields. During times of arroyo cutting, however, the water drains away quickly down Chaco Wash, providing no benefit for farming.

Two important sources of runoff, in very different ways, are the mesas bordering the north and south sides of the canyon. On the north, the mesa top above the cliff face is a wide bench with large expanses of bedrock and thin soil, whereas the mesa on the south presents a series of short, stepped and broken terraces, many with heavy soils. When moisture is sufficient to produce runoff, much of the flow on the north moves with considerable velocity across the bedrock and into short side-canyon arroyos that drain into Chaco Wash. Surface flow on the south runs more slowly and is absorbed into terrace benches, talus slopes, and the bottoms of side canyons. The differences are starkly reflected today on the two sides of Chaco Canyon. Almost every side canyon on the north has a narrow, deep arroyo, but there are virtually no arroyos on the south.

Because Puebloan farmers survived only by being acutely aware of their environment, they undoubtedly recognized the south side of Chaco Canyon as offering greater potential for simple farming techniques. There they found terrace benches well suited for small plots of corn, while the bottoms of side canyons were ideal for *akchin* (floodwater) farming. Sand dunes in places such as Werito's Rincon offered an additional micro-niche for planting beans, a method that was fully developed by the Hopi people to the west. And winter snow melts more slowly on the south side of the canyon, percolating deep into the soil to provide vital moisture for germinating seeds in the spring.

Tom Windes's long-term collection of rain-gauge data in and around Chaco Canyon indicates that there was an additional benefit to farming on the south of Chaco Wash. He discovered that when summer storms move from the southwest toward the canyon and meet Chacra Mesa, they are deflected into breaks or gaps in that barrier. This funneling, he found, tends to hold storms in the gaps for longer periods of time, resulting in much greater precipitation. This could explain why Steve Lekson's "downtown Chaco," a dense concentration of great houses and small-house sites, is situated near the break called South Gap.

Figure 2.4. A Navajo cornfield in Mockingbird Canyon, on the north side of Chaco Wash, in the early twentieth century.

Some Chacoan farmers soon learned that if they were to take advantage of the full agricultural potential of the north side of the canyon, they had to capture water flowing off the mesa top and divert it to fields. I spent a full year in Chaco investigating ancient farming practices and located systems for capturing water in seventeen of the twenty-eight side canyons between Wijiji on the east and Peñasco Blanco on the west. My team and I also discovered water management features on the south side of the canyon, near Casa Rinconada and Peñasco Blanco, respectively. We were certain that undiscovered systems must lie in the other rincons on the north side of the canyon.

The north-side farmers were remarkably consistent in the ways they collected, diverted, and spread the water that flowed off the slickrock and into short side canyons. They constructed earthen or masonry diversion dams near the mouths of these drainages to channel the runoff into canals. At the ends of the canals they built headgates to further channel the floodwater onto fields. To ensure that all plants received equal water, the farmers gridded their fields into rectangular plots separated by low earth borders. Through the use of aerial photographs, we were able to identify several farms near Chetro Ketl that had individual garden plots averaging seventy-five by forty-five feet.

Social Adaptations to Food Shortages

Chacoans also used social strategies to deal with potential food shortages. Usually, ancestral Puebloans responded to impending famine by moving to better farming areas. This happened occasionally at Chaco, particularly after 1080 CE, but people never fully abandoned Chaco Canyon at any time between 500 and 1150 CE. Instead, they seem to have successfully used ancient systems of organizing kin to good effect in certain canyon microenvironments. Evidence of two contrasting strategies may be reflected in the predominance of small-house sites on the south side of the canyon and of great houses on the north. Linda Cordell's analysis of Pueblo farming suggests a reason for this difference.

She proposes that Pueblo peoples practiced both labor-intensive and land- and time-intensive farming. In labor-intensive systems, well-coordinated and often large groups of workers constructed and maintained soil- and water-control facilities in fairly restricted areas. Land- and time-intensive systems were less technologically sophisticated, and smaller work groups often spent more time in larger areas of scattered plots practicing overplanting, multiple planting, fallowing, and shifting cultivation.

Chacoans living in small-house sites found the many micro-niche locations for fields on the south

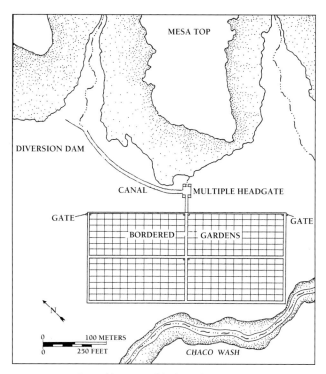

Figure 2.5. Plan of large gridded gardens using captured runoff from the north side of the canyon.

side of the canyon ideal for land- and time-intensive farming practices, and the dispersed nature of these sites suggests a social system based on extended families. On the other hand, the need for controlling and diverting large amounts of floodwater to gridded fields on the north side of the canyon would have demanded a more labor-intensive system. Efficiency may be gained by concentrating labor, and the few great houses along the northern margins of the canyon probably were organized in a way that permitted the clustering of larger social groups. Great-house farmers might have been organized like residents of the contemporary Tewa pueblos, where governing power is shared by two separate but equal groups.

The farming methods practiced by small-house groups were widespread and had deep Puebloan roots. Yet the great-house populations successfully developed farming based on water control in Chaco Canyon over the course of three centuries. The same formality that characterized their north-side farms is evident in great-house planning, and I believe changes in those plans over time may denote the responses of great-house groups to an altered environment.

The earliest ninth-century canyon great houses were larger than contemporaneous small-house sites,

and their plans held embryonic hints of the "classic" D-shape so common in eleventh-century buildings. These structures were situated across from "funnel" zones in Chacra Mesa so that farmers could take advantage of increased rainfall and floodwaters entering the canyon through these breaks. By forestalling arroyo cutting, the dune dam below Peñasco Blanco also enhanced the value of bottomland farms. The earliest great-house farmers undoubtedly experimented with simple water-control devices, but these were probably designed more to spread water than to channel it. At the same time, small-house communities across the canyon practiced more traditional forms of planting.

By narrowing their farming methods, great-house farmers limited their options for adjusting to the breaching of the dune dam and a new cycle of arroyo cutting around 900 CE. Farmers in Chaco benefited from the regionwide gradual increase in moisture in the early tenth century, but entrenchment of Chaco Wash placed great-house floodwater fields in jeopardy because side tributaries eroded to the base of the main channel, lowering the water table and flushing water directly into the central wash. Great-house farmers did not experience the effects of this process immediately, but gradual headwater erosion of Chaco Wash ultimately threatened the farms near their clustered communities. Early expressions of the classic great-house plan, such as at Pueblo Bonito, seem to have become frozen in place for almost a century, a period Lekson describes as "the hiatus." Small-house farmers were less severely affected because hydrologic and geomorphic conditions on the south side of the canyon resisted arroyo cutting.

In the eleventh century, as precipitation increased and water tables rose, Puebloans once again found Chaco Canyon an attractive place to farm. A return to channel filling might have been hastened and possibly even initiated when Chacoans built a masonry dam in the breached dune below Peñasco Blanco. Though it created a playa or possibly a shallow lake, it might not have been especially useful for crops. Instead, it may have been built to restore canyon bottomlands to a condition remembered from times past. This was a time when great-house groups invested heavily in water-control structures despite the occasional destruction of headgates and canals by flooding. The enlargement

Figure 2.6. Chaco Wash.

of older great houses and the establishment of several new ones, all reaching the architectural apogee of the classic great-house form, mirrored good times in Chaco. Small-house groups benefited from increased rainfall, too, continuing their practice of multiple micro-niche farming. Growing communities, however, may have begun to use up all suitable canyon farmland by the mid-eleventh century, and several new great houses, such as Pueblo Pintado and Kin Klizhin, were established outside the canyon's boundaries.

The Final Decades

Movement beyond the canyon could also have been stimulated by a two-decade dry period that started around 1080 CE, though a stable water table and continued channel filling lessened its impact. These unsettling times were followed around 1100 by three decades of much greater precipitation. I believe this may have lulled some Chacoan farmers into complacency, because it was accompanied by a surge in great-house construction. Apparently, though, not everyone believed prosperity would continue, for between about 1080 and 1140 groups from Chaco Canyon established several large Chacoan great houses in the San Juan River valley, including Salmon and the West Ruin at Aztec. Chacoan concerns about the future were well founded, for a major drought that began around 1130 and lasted, with only a minor

break, for fifty years underscored the harsh realities of depending on rainfall.

This event ultimately proved too taxing for the Chacoan farmers and triggered the abandonment of Chaco Canyon by the late twelfth century. By 1150, only small patches of stunted maize were being tended in the Chacra Mesa. This ribbon of life in the inner San Juan Basin had sheltered and sustained its Puebloan occupants for more than six hundred years, providing them a toehold of existence within a sea of desert uniformity. Though their isolation forced Chacoans to travel great distances—to the margins of the basin—for many of the resources they came to need, they had successfully farmed the canyon through tenacity, experimentation, and an occasional stroke of luck such as the dune dam.

The challenges faced by the people of Chaco sparked the genesis of their culture and then propelled them through centuries of often spectacular growth. In the end, the failing clouds, the drying winds, and the heat of summer prevailed, and the canyon returned to the way it was before.

R. Gwinn Vivian is curator emeritus at Arizona State University in Tucson. A longtime researcher of Chaco Canyon and author of *The Chacoan Prehistory of the San Juan Basin*, he is particularly interested in how the people of Chaco adapted to their arid environment.

Figure 3.1. Looking west down the Chaco River at sunset from a Puebloan shrine overlooking Casa del Rio, an early Chacoan great house.

The Rise of Early Chacoan Great Houses

Thomas C. Windes

While many people have expressed great interest in what ultimately happened to the people of Chaco to bring about its demise, others' curiosity has been piqued by how their odyssey began. Some researchers believe that faraway Mesoamericans brought this intriguing culture to prominence. Others contend that societal stress and competition for scarce resources enabled some leaders to become powerful enough to create the complex stratified society responsible for the multistory stone buildings, or great houses, whose ruins still impress.

Chaco's beginnings remain unclear, but we do know that the society coalesced around 1040 or 1050 CE and soon afterward reached a peak of widespread influence and power. This was a time when the Chacoan leaders mobilized labor on a large scale to construct great kivas, roads, an intricate communications system, and new great houses, while refurbishing older great houses. They also imported a variety of goods including pottery, prized stone for flaking, timbers, turquoise, seashells, copper bells, and macaws. The remnants of much of these goods were eventually deposited in large heaps in front of the great houses.

For the early decades, these heaps appear to represent domestic refuse. But in deposits from the middle of the eleventh century, there is little domestic trash such as ash, charcoal, and plant remains, for the great houses were becoming buildings with few permanent residents. Nevertheless, the enormous quantities of refuse at these sites distinguish them from the normal Puebloan pattern of settlement and offer testimony that unusual activities were carried out at the early great houses. This is especially the case for those situated along the Chaco River, a watercourse distinct from the incised Chaco Wash within the confines of Chaco Canyon proper.

Although archaeologists remain uncertain about what caused the rise of Chacoan culture and even when it became a distinct entity, I believe Chaco Canyon was exerting its pull as early as the late 400s CE. At that time, Puebloan farmers built two large pithouse villages, now known as Shabik'eshchee and 29SJ423, one at either end of the present-day national park. The sites spanned a one- to two-mile-long strip starting at the canyon bottom and running over Chacra Mesa on the south side of the canyon and down into the southern plains. It was an unusual settlement plan and an ambitious enterprise, for each village incorporated more than a hundred semi-subterranean pithouses used for residences, as well as a community great kiva. Residents may have used these villages only seasonally, living elsewhere during part of the year. Such a pattern, indeed, may always have characterized life in Chaco Canyon. Nevertheless, in comparison with other, contemporaneous settlements in the greater San Juan Basin, these two villages were unusual in size, layout, presence of community buildings, and density of refuse, characteristics that seem to foreshadow what was to come centuries later.

After nearly a century of occupation, the inhabitants of Shabik'eshchee and 29SJ423 departed, leaving behind the burned remains of their great kivas. There is still much to learn about these villages, but they must be considered prime pathways for later Chaco Canyon developments.

Early Immigrants from the South

Centuries later, around 800 CE, many families from the southern San Juan Basin, near present-day Grants, New Mexico, moved north to two locations just outside Chaco Canyon. One group established a settlement of clustered houses along the south fork of Fajada Wash, and another group, of which little is known, formed a village in the next drainage valley to the west. The newcomers established residences that, although scattered, were clustered within a small area, replicating the clustered great-house settlement pattern of a century later. All the while, the population of nearby Chaco Canyon was living in a few widely scattered hamlets.

Several aspects of these two new settlements close to the canyon deserve mention, particularly the well-studied village along the south fork of Fajada Wash. Both have shallow middens, or refuse scatters, that contain high percentages of chipped stone and pottery imported from far away, and both have clear views of two prominent topographical features—Fajada Butte and Huérfano Mountain. These landmarks later became significant: Fajada Butte for its well-known solstice marker and Huérfano Mountain as an important link in Chaco's shrine communication network.

Of the twenty-seven houses in the south fork village, only two adjacent structures were built of stone masonry rather than the traditional mud, and they could be seen from every other house in the settlement. In addition, a short road connected these two stone houses to a nearby great kiva. This village is the earliest site known in the vicinity of Chaco Canyon that might be designated a great-house settlement, though it pales in comparison with those that came just a little later west of the canyon.

For unexplainable reasons, these two early settlements close to Chaco Canyon were abandoned after a mere decade or so of occupation. Their location in one of the driest areas of the region, now treeless and waterless, might have helped influence the settlers' decision to leave. In addition, although better locations exist within the canyon, the villagers appear to have left the area altogether, perhaps because new, more fertile land was unavailable or because of social resistance from the canyon residents.

The Rise of Stone Masonry Architecture in the 800s

During the Pueblo I period, in the 700s and 800s CE, the inhabitants of the San Juan Basin surrounding Chaco Canyon generally lived in scattered dwellings big enough for one or two families, which they usually occupied for less than a decade or two. By the late 800s, dense clusters of people were again living in large villages with communal buildings, primarily along the northern tributaries of the San Juan River, which flows south from the melted snowpack of the nearby Colorado mountains. At this time, most Pueblo people built their houses of adobe or jacal—upright poles tied together and plastered with mud—constructions that deteriorate quickly without constant upkeep. Some residents of the northern villages, however, began to experiment with stone masonry.

Archaeological excavations conducted in the 1980s, prior to the filling of Dolores Reservoir north of Mesa Verde, revealed one of the best known of these northern sites—McPhee Village. The principal house within the village, known as McPhee Pueblo, was built between about 780 and 860 CE. It initially consisted of twenty to twenty-five rooms built in a crescent shape with jacal walls set on sandstone slab footings. Its crescentic plan was common to the era and across the Colorado Plateau.

Beginning around 860, McPhee Pueblo's inhabitants became innovative. Using stone masonry construction methods, they enlarged their living quarters to about one hundred rooms, which they formed in two joined, crescent-shaped roomblocks. Now they had an apartment large enough to house eighteen to twenty families totaling about a hundred people. Within it, a large central stone pithouse—not a great kiva—became the focal point for special community activities and rituals. Either because of an unusually long settlement period or because events focused at the pueblo attracted others, or for both reasons, the outside midden became abnormally large, reaching more than three feet in depth.

In architectural form, McPhee Pueblo displays remarkable similarities to certain great houses, such as Peñasco Blanco, Pueblo Bonito, and Una Vida, that were under construction a few years later in Chaco Canyon and elsewhere in the San Juan Basin. The similarities are apparent in general layout, large

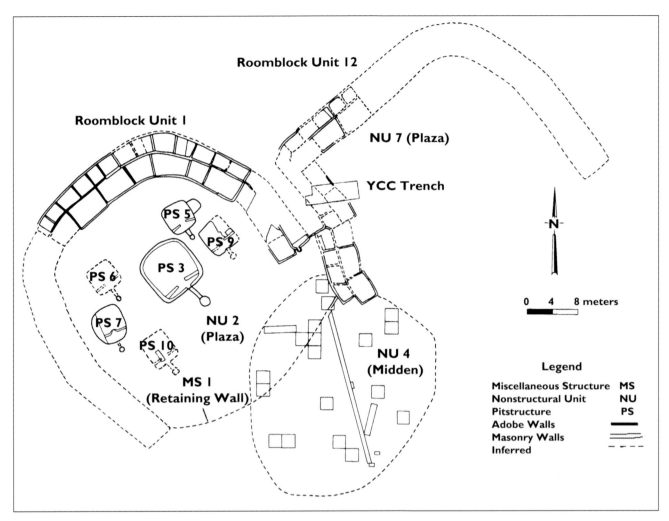

Figure 3.2. Plan of McPhee Pueblo.

room sizes, construction materials and techniques, construction timing, and refuse deposition. Despite the small numbers and widespread locations of excavated, dated tree-ring samples from these sites, the coincidence of construction at McPhee, Bonito, and Una Vida is remarkable: at least one episode in the collection of beams for construction at all three took place in the same year, 861. McPhee, of course, housed many more people than either Peñasco Blanco, Pueblo Bonito, or Una Vida. Still, if archaeologists had found this site in Chaco Canyon, they would certainly have classified it as an early great house.

In the higher locations around the San Juan Basin, such as the Dolores area, rainfall and snowfall were greater than at lower elevations by a factor of two or three to one, but the higher elevations experienced shorter growing seasons. When farming in the higher elevations around the periphery of the San Juan Basin became untenable around 875 CE, many people moved to lower elevations where the growing seasons were longer. At the same time, in the central basin, a new type of structure appeared—the great house with its commanding setting, substantial stone architecture, and massing of refuse, but without the great kiva community structure. Instead, the new great houses might have continued the McPhee Pueblo–style giant pithouse as the community center, although excavation would be needed to confirm this conjecture.

These impressive stone buildings mark a new social dynamic in the basin interior. Clearly, these great houses held an irresistible attraction for the new immigrants. Exactly what the appeal was will require more study, but it must have gone beyond the lure of a longer growing season. Archaeological evidence

Figure 3.3a. Room in McPhee Pueblo, about 860 CE.

Figure 3.3b. Room in old section of Pueblo Bonito, about 875 CE.

even in the driest years, lies just below the surface of the sandy washes and provides reliable places for farming. It is along this route that we find the remains of many of the earliest San Juan Basin great houses.

Expansion along the Chaco River

Not surprisingly, past researchers have failed to recognize that many impressive house mounds in the San Juan Basin were actually precursors of the great houses in the canyon core. Whereas Peñasco Blanco, Pueblo Bonito, and Una Vida have often been cited as the probable progenitors of the Chacoan story, it is my view that many other, more obscure sites in the interior San Juan Basin were the true earliest great houses.

Dating to the late 800s and 900s, these sites are concentrated along the sixty-two-mile Chaco River corridor between Shiprock, New Mexico, and Chaco Canyon. The shallow water table and the broad expanse of riverbed might have provided the best opportunity for successful food production within the dry, unpredictable interior of the basin. The large numbers of food-processing tools found at these sites are testament to local farming success. Surplus food, of course, would have been a major attraction for those living in other areas, who relied on the usual unpredictable rainfall for their crops.

now offers a clue: many of the houses the highlanders left behind were intentionally burned, a practice exceedingly rare in the interior basin. Intentional burning can suggest strife or ritualized abandonment. Perhaps, in addition to increased farming potential, the interior offered people opportunities for a more peaceful new life, away from land disputes and village factionalism.

Whatever the draw, migrants traveled along the broad Chaco River and its tributaries, where water,

The site of Casa del Rio, for example, located along the Chaco River a mere five miles downstream from Peñasco Blanco, includes a stone masonry great house of twenty to twenty-eight rooms that housed perhaps four families. Dating to the late 800s, this building overlies a gigantic, slightly earlier adobe Pueblo I structure that housed as many as sixteen families. Although a great amount of refuse was tossed in front of the Pueblo I dwelling, the later great-house refuse is more impressive: it rises sixteen

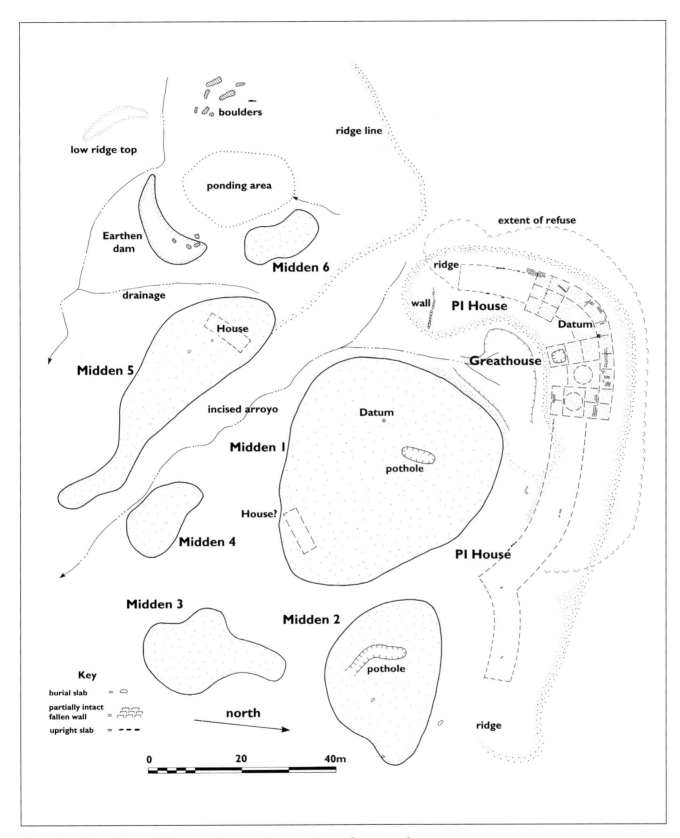

boulders

ridge line

low ridge top

ponding area

extent of refuse

Earthen dam

ridge

wall

PI House

Midden 6

Datum

drainage

House

Midden 5

Greathouse

incised arroyo

Datum

Midden 1

pothole

House?

PI House

Midden 4

Midden 3

Midden 2

pothole

Key

burial slab   =

partially intact
fallen wall   =

upright slab   = ‒ ‒ ‒

north

ridge

0   20   40m

Figure 3.4. Plan of Casa del Rio great house and surrounding refuse mounds.

Figure 3.5. Aerial view of Peñasco Blanco and Chaco Canyon, looking east.

feet above the surrounding terrain, makes up an estimated 2,230 cubic yards, and is visible for miles around. What is more, Casa del Rio is the nexus of several prehistoric roads and is in a direct line of sight to a nearby communication shrine, one that also forms a link directly to Peñasco Blanco and the rest of the canyon network.

Other early stone masonry houses along the Chaco River, such as Lake Valley, Willow Canyon, and Great Bend, also yield impressive heaps of masonry with massive midden deposits. I suggest that such prodigious deposits represent periodic gatherings of outsiders who engaged in political or ritual events and in the distribution of food, trade, feasting, and purely social interactions. Where did these participants come from? Discarded pottery vessels and flaked stones indicate that many such

items were carried from the slopes of the Chuska Mountains. A prehistoric road appears to have connected all these river communities with the Chuskas, an indication of the importance of the Chuska area to the expanding settlement along the Chaco River.

The Early Great Houses of Chaco Canyon
Of the five large stone masonry structures erected in Chaco Canyon proper in the mid- to late 800s, three saw later expansion into the huge, multistory, stone masonry buildings of Peñasco Blanco, Pueblo Bonito, and Una Vida. These great houses stand out because they were taller and more massive than any other structures on the ninth-century Southwestern landscape. Still, they retained the crescentic layout typical of contemporary Puebloan habitations of the period.

In the mid- to late 1000s, a highly visible and appealing type of architecture came into vogue. It included core-and-veneer masonry, up to four stories (possibly five at Pueblo Bonito), kivas built within the house construction, a great kiva in the plaza or nearby, and a large mound or midden. In one case, that of Pueblo Bonito, the mound was leveled to serve for a short time as a walled platform. Generations of anthropology field-school students, many of whom later became professional archaeologists, regarded these architectural monuments as the beginning of the Chacoan story. Today, we realize that they represent not its beginning but its culmination.

New View of Chaco's Origins

To summarize, it is my view that the ancestral Pueblo people of the Four Corners region built their first great houses in the Dolores River area of southwestern Colorado and elsewhere in the 800s. Sometime around 875, during a period of great environmental stress, failing food production and the inevitable social disharmony forced many of these people in the higher elevations to relocate. Some settled to the south along the Chaco River and other tributaries of the San Juan, where they built early versions of the later classic Chacoan great houses. These sites, particularly those along the Chaco River but not yet in the canyon, became focal points for large gatherings of people who came from around the basin. They might also have served to bond the scattered San Juan Basin communities and link people, in memory at least, to their former homelands.

Other large and small great houses along the tributaries of the Chaco River—Kin Bineola, Pueblo Bonito, Una Vida, and East Community, for example—lack significant amounts of refuse from this early period, even though large settlements of people were living in small houses nearby. Later, for a short time in the mid-eleventh century, a new social order arose, and political and ritual power was concentrated around Pueblo Bonito. By this time, the earlier great houses such as Casa del Rio had seen the last of their large gatherings, and the focus had shifted to downtown Chaco Canyon.

Acknowledgments

I thank the many volunteers who helped me reinvestigate the Chaco River houses and provided assistance for many other avenues of this investigation. My very special thanks go to Eileen Bacha for editorial and field assistance.

Thomas C. Windes has worked as an archaeologist for the National Park Service for thirty-two years, doing research on the Chaco culture. His interests cover chronometric dating (dendrochronology and archaeomagnetism), wood production, ceramics, ground stone, ornaments, field methodology, the environment, and settlement.

Figure 4.1. North wall of Pueblo Bonito, 1929.

Architecture

The Central Matter of Chaco Canyon

Stephen H. Lekson

Architecture is the central matter of Chaco Canyon. Its major ruins make Chaco distinctive, perhaps unique. Our understanding of Chacoan architecture follows directly upon the history of research at this ancestral Pueblo center.

It was the remarkable size of some ruins in Chaco Canyon that first attracted archaeological attention. Chaco's giant "great houses," built of banded masonry and shaped like huge Ds, Es, Os, and Ls, lured the pioneer archaeologist Richard Wetherill away from Mesa Verde. He moved to Chaco, promoted its archaeology, and ultimately led the first major excavations in 1896 at Pueblo Bonito. The work was sponsored by the American Museum of Natural History.

Pueblo Bonito's archaeology was spectacular. The building itself was monumental, and it contained treasures rarely seen in the ancestral Pueblo ("Anasazi") region. Tribal wars broke out between the American Museum, the Museum of New Mexico, the Smithsonian, and other institutions vying for excavation rights at Chaco great houses. Throughout the first half of the twentieth century, the archaeology of Chaco Canyon was fragmented into independent projects at various sites.

Professional rivalries adversely affected the science: excavators sometimes published accounts of their work with little or no reference to other projects. And so each great house was seen as a separate entity: Pueblo Bonito and Chetro Ketl must have been independent towns, much like the Pueblo villages of New Mexico and Arizona. The Pueblo Indians share cultures, ceremonies, economies,

and architectural traditions, but each Native town in the Southwest is a separate social unit.

Before the development of tree-ring dating, the great houses were assumed to have been of the "Great Pueblo" period, the thirteenth-century climax of the Four Corners Puebloan culture, which included the cliff dwellings of Mesa Verde, Hovenweep, and many other famous sites. Chacoan great houses were larger and better built than the cliff dwellings. Perhaps Chaco was the climax of the climax? Tree rings, however, revealed that Chaco's great houses were built much earlier than the sites on Mesa Verde. Cliff Palace was built about 1250 to 1280 CE, but construction at Pueblo Bonito began about 875 and ended at 1130.

Chaco's great houses were built more than a century earlier than the Great Pueblo period. Indeed, great houses—with hundreds of rooms, massive masonry, and geometrically formal ground plans—were built at a time when the typical family house consisted of an earth-covered pit structure and a small, almost ephemeral "pueblo" of five or six rooms. More than 90 percent of Pueblo people, during the Chaco era, lived in these serviceable but unimpressive small houses. The contrast between small and great houses was so remarkable that some archaeologists believed the two architectural traditions represented two distinct cultures or ethnic groups.

Why were great houses so unlike other Pueblo buildings of Chaco's time? Why were great houses concentrated in Chaco Canyon? Was Chaco more than a valley filled with pueblos?

Figure 4.2. Artist's reconstruction of a typical Pueblo I small house. This design, consisting of an arc of rooms and a ramada with a pit structure in front, was common to ancestral Pueblo dwellings throughout the Four Corners region for many generations (see also fig. 3.2). The form is reflected in the earliest construction of Pueblo Bonito.

By 1960, the institutional rivalries surrounding Chaco had faded into footnotes, and it was possible for archaeologists to consider the canyon as a whole. The whole was much more than the sum of its parts. In 1965, Gordon Vivian, Tom Mathews, and Bryant Bannister summarized the archaeology of Chaco Canyon in two separate studies, bound together as "Southwestern Monuments Association Technical Series no. 6." Vivian and Mathews, in their report, *Kin Kletso: A Pueblo III Community in Chaco Canyon*, described three different kinds of architecture: first, a dozen great houses (which they called the "Bonito phase"); second, scores of small houses comparable to regular Puebloan construction of the time (the "Hosta Butte phase," named for a prominent landmark); and third, a small group of late great houses that reflected Mesa Verde styles (the "McElmo phase," the term used at Mesa Verde for the period just before Cliff Palace). Bannister's *Tree Ring Dating of Archaeological Sites in the Chaco Canyon Region, New Mexico*, synthesized and reevaluated the tree-ring dates known from Chaco sites and offered the first site-by-site descriptions of all the excavated Chaco ruins. The tree-ring dates showed that the three phases—Bonito, Hosta Butte and McElmo—were all contemporaneous. That is, at about 1100, Chaco had three notably different architectures: great-house, McElmo, and small-house styles. Chaco was a complicated place.

These two studies stood for decades as the definitive summary of Chaco archaeology (and the volume remains remarkably useful even today). When I began to study Chaco archaeology in the mid-1970s, Vivian, Mathews, and Bannister was the standard reference. At that time, the National Park Service's Chaco Project was several years into a long program of excavations and research. That work reemphasized Chaco's unusual and perhaps unique place in Southwestern prehistory.

In the 1970s, after surveying the entire canyon and producing more accurate maps of the great houses, Alden Hayes, then field director of the Chaco Project, produced the first major reevaluation of Chaco archaeology. Hayes was so impressed with great-house architecture that in his 1981 report he concluded that overlords or agents from the high civilizations of ancient Mexico had traveled to Chaco and transformed local Pueblo architectural traditions into a new great-house style. Many of Hayes's professional colleagues shared his view. The next task of the Chaco Project was to excavate a great house and test Hayes's theory.

I became part of a new staff hired for this major undertaking. Our duties only began with pick and shovel; in winter we analyzed artifacts and wrote reports. Assigned the topic of great-house architecture, I revisited Vivian and Mathews's report. And I took advantage of all the new data—Hayes's great-house maps, new tree-ring dates, newly published reports on Pueblo Bonito, Chetro Ketl, and other sites—and the opportunity to spend time in Chaco Canyon examining the ruins. With much help from

Figure 4.3. Early Pueblo Bonito wall in foreground with later core-and-veneer wall behind it.

cally new forms. Whereas traditional Pueblo dwellings had small rooms, low ceilings, and only a single story, Pueblo Bonito at 850–900 CE had large rooms, tall ceilings, and as many as three stories. An entire Chacoan small house could fit into a single room at Pueblo Bonito. But the masonry generally used for small houses was unsuited to the much larger dimensions of great houses.

An early wall around the rear of Pueblo Bonito, built in the early 900s in the old-fashioned way, began to buckle and fail. In about 1020, Chacoan builders saved the old wall by surrounding it with another wall, using a new masonry style. It worked. At Pueblo Bonito, you can almost see the Chaco builders experimenting with masonry and, over several decades, developing the massive, superbly crafted Chacoan walls that distinguish great houses of the eleventh and twelfth centuries from previous buildings. This, I thought, showed that great houses were a local phenomenon rather than a Mexican import. The Chacoans invented the new masonry styles in order to build bigger buildings.

But why build big buildings in the first place? What were great houses? The masonry was local,

many colleagues, I wrote *Great Pueblo Architecture of Chaco Canyon*, published by the Park Service in 1984, twenty years after the Vivian, Mathews, and Bannister volume.

My conclusions fell more in line with those of Vivian, Mathews, and Bannister than with those of Alden Hayes, who nevertheless read my "schoolboy" drafts with patience and redirected my wilder fancies with wisdom. I argued that Chacoan architecture developed from regional Pueblo, not Mexican, traditions. The earliest building at Pueblo Bonito used standard Pueblo masonry of its time to create radi-

but Hayes was right: great houses were astonishingly unlike other ancestral Pueblo buildings. Recall that when great houses were at their peak around 1100, almost everyone else in the Pueblo Southwest was living in small houses of half a dozen rooms and a deep pit-structure, or "kiva." Pueblo Bonito by then covered almost two and a half acres (106,800 square feet), rose to five stories, and had at least seven hundred rooms and forty kivas or pit structures. A precisely sited north-south wall divided Bonito's vast enclosed plaza in two, with one enormous great kiva in each half. A large ponderosa pine in the west plaza must have been watered and encouraged to grow, for it was far out of its natural range; presumably, the tree had powerful symbolic value. Just south of the main building, two rectangular platform mounds, each the size of a basketball court, rose five or six feet above a surrounding network of roads, compound walls, and other esoteric architecture. We do not know what structures the Bonitoans might have built atop these massive platforms.

Chetro Ketl, with perhaps six hundred rooms, was comparable in size to Pueblo Bonito. A colonnade faced its plaza (see fig. 7.4, p. 51). Colonnades were not traditional Puebloan architectural elements—they occur only at Chaco and in Mexico. Four other great houses at Chaco Canyon were built on this expansive scale: Una Vida, Peñasco Blanco, Pueblo del Arroyo, and Pueblo Alto. Other great houses were smaller, but still mammoth compared with small houses.

Pueblo Bonito and the two other earliest great houses (Peñasco Blanco and Una Vida) began, in the late ninth and early tenth centuries, as monumentally "scaled up" versions of contemporary ancestral Pueblo houses. That is, the plan of early Pueblo Bonito resembled a line of regular small-house family dwellings, side by side, but vastly larger and multistoried. After these beginnings, great-house architecture diverged increasingly from contemporary small sites. By 1130, later great houses, such as Kin Kletso, looked very different indeed from the six-rooms-and-a-kiva standard ancestral Pueblo home.

Tom Windes directed Chaco Project excavations at Pueblo Alto. The Chacoans built this large great house—before excavating it, we assumed it stood three stories high—on the north mesa, three hundred feet above Pueblo Bonito and Chetro Ketl on the canyon floor. Its view extended from the mountains behind Albuquerque to the peaks behind Mesa Verde. Windes discovered that Pueblo Alto was only one story high (though ceiling heights were impressively tall, some more than twelve feet), and despite its 135 rooms, only a few families had lived there. He based the latter conclusion on the absence of features such as fire boxes and storage bins, the marks of everyday domestic use, in most of the rooms at the site. Extending his analysis to Pueblo Bonito and Chetro Ketl, he concluded that few of the great

houses, if any, were "pueblos"—that is, they were not towns filled with families.

I reached similar conclusions from another line of evidence: pit structures. Circular, underground rooms at both great houses and small houses are conventionally called kivas, after the ceremonial structures we see today in the plazas of Pueblo Indian villages. Rio Grande pueblos typically have one or two kivas apiece, continuing the pattern seen at scores of ruins from the fourteenth century onward. Rio Grande kivas are probably modern versions of the great kivas at Chaco, which usually had one or two great kivas per great-house community. Archaeologists seek the "pit house to kiva" transition like a holy grail, but perhaps it never happened. Great kivas were there from the beginning, and great kivas are still there today in the plazas of modern pueblos.

What, then, are all the little "kivas" at Chaco and other ancient sites? The scores of small, circular rooms at Chaco and Mesa Verde probably were not kivas like those at modern pueblos but instead the final and most elaborate form of the pit house. Pit houses—circular or square underground rooms—were the primary residential structures of ancestral Pueblo peoples for at least five centuries before Chaco. They were easy to build, cool in the summer, and warm in the cold desert winters. After about 900 CE, people began to add small aboveground structures behind the pit houses; eventually those small sites evolved into the pueblos of today. But at modern Rio Grande pueblos, there are hundreds of rooms for each kiva. Recall that, at Chaco's time, a typical small house consisted of only five or six rooms and a pit structure ("kiva"). At Yellow Jacket, the largest Mesa Verde pueblo, that ratio was even lower: three rooms per pit structure. With almost two hundred "kivas," Yellow Jacket has been interpreted as a ceremonial center, but the same interpretation could be applied uniformly across the Chaco and Great Pueblo periods: almost every large site had many "kivas" compared with relatively few rooms.

If the small, circular pit structures were actually houses (or rather, parts of small houses), then we can estimate the number of families living in a great house by its number of original "kivas." (Later reoccupations of great houses often added more "kivas,"

Figure 4.4. View of the southeast section of Pueblo Bonito, showing a series of circular and rectangular rooms.

or pit houses). At Pueblo Alto, there were six or seven original "kivas," and this number supports Windes's conclusion: few families lived in Pueblo Alto or other great houses.

The low room-to-"kiva" ratio is reversed at some great houses, where a circular pit structure might be associated with thirty or more rooms. Families living in great houses had many more rooms and much more floor area than did other ancestral Pueblo families. The great houses' hundreds of extra rooms and thousands of square feet represented something more than domestic households. Recent analyses by Jill Neitzel suggest that Pueblo Bonito was an elite residence—that is, the home of a small group of families who were politically, socially, or ceremonially more powerful than other people in the region and who demonstrated their importance by living in very large houses. They lived in large, elaborate pit houses with suites or apartments of perhaps a dozen rooms attached—rather like a traditional small house, but much bigger.

Housing was only a portion of each great house. Scores of other, nonresidential rooms probably served a variety of purposes: storage (approaching warehouse dimensions), chambers reserved for ceremonial or political functions, temporary housing for visitors or laborers. Elsewhere, I have referred to the Chacoan great houses as "palaces," a word that reflects their multiple functions as elite residences, warehouses, administrative offices, and ceremonial centers. Indeed, Chacoan great houses are comparable in size and complexity to the famous Minoan palaces of Crete. This is not to say that Chacoan society rivaled or even resembled that of ancient Crete; great houses were very modest palaces in almost every regard.

In the early 1980s, I attempted to estimate the amount of labor required to build great houses, from digging mortar and shaping stones to building walls. I concluded that great-house construction required about forty thousand person hours of building labor every year between 1050 and 1125. This must have come not from the great-house residents but from outside. Those who lived in the buildings organized and planned but did not labor.

Some great-house building may have been principally for the purpose of massing. "Massing" is an architectural term that the archaeologist John Stein and others employ to suggest that the Chacoans built great houses to create impressive forms. At Pueblo

Figure 4.5. Large, deep nonresidential rooms in Pueblo Bonito may have been used for bulk storage.

Bonito, for example, most of the building consisted of dark interior spaces, deep below multiple upper stories and far removed from plaza-front doorways. Some of these rooms could have been used to store all sorts of objects, as Pueblo people do today, but it seems likely that the creation of impressive, monumental forms was also a motivation.

The McElmo phase, late in Chaco's history, is a case in point. John Stein and Ruth Van Dyke have suggested that the compact McElmo structures (see fig. 1.5) of the early 1100s represent pure massing—that is, building to build. With their small, compact rooms and multiple stories, McElmo buildings stick up on the landscape almost like towers. They show little evidence of any kind of use; most, in fact, have only one or two "kivas" (presumably indicating only one or two families in residence) and no trash middens. The final spurt of Chacoan building created mass as well as more monuments on the Chacoan landscape.

The large, geometrically formal great houses were meant to be seen and to create an impression from the cliffs above Pueblo Bonito and Chetro Ketl and from the "roads" on the valley bottom. Their layout demonstrates canons or rules in construction and form, just as medieval cathedrals or Buddhist stupas have common features, ground plans, and geometries. Anna Sofaer, John Stein, and other researchers have begun to unravel those rules.

After a hundred years of scientific research in Chaco, we are recognizing that it was more than a canyon full of pueblos. It was an architectural composition, combining a dozen great houses and scores of other monumental features with a distinctive, even unique landscape to create a small planned city. When I introduced the term "downtown Chaco" in 1981 for the complex of buildings around Pueblo Bonito, Chetro Ketl, and Pueblo Alto, I was not the first to suggest that Chaco was formally designed. In 1978, John Fritz demonstrated that downtown Chaco reflected two major axes: a perfect north-south meridian from Pueblo Alto on the north to Tsin Kletsin on the south, and an east-west axis from Pueblo Bonito to Chetro Ketl. Gwinn Vivian and later

Tom Windes carefully mapped the dense nexus of roads and stairways that connected Pueblo Alto, Pueblo Bonito, and Chetro Ketl, and John Stein and his colleagues extended that constructed landscape to encompass all of downtown Chaco and beyond. Stein, working with Richard Friedman, Taft Blackhorse, and others, now posits a sculpted Chaco with great houses, complexes of pyramid-like platforms, roads, broad ramps and stairways, massive walls enclosing whole districts of buildings, and an astonishing variety of other monumental features. Interspersed among all these structures was a complex series of irrigation systems and gardens. Taken together, the built environment of Chaco resembles, in conception if not in scale, the ceremonial centers of ancient Mexico and the Maya region.

Stein and his colleagues and Anna Sofaer have explored the layout of downtown Chaco, around Pueblo Bonito and Chetro Ketl, showing that the whole area was almost theaterlike as a setting for pomp and circumstance, ritual and procession. The flat, featureless ground between Pueblo Bonito and Chetro Ketl may have been a central stage for ritual; Stein and his colleagues suggest that the canyon walls there had distinctive acoustical properties that magnified the sounds of ceremony. The canyon's rim provided unmatched viewing for hundreds, even thousands, of observers, perhaps pilgrims reaching the canyon on the ceremonial roads. The terraced roofs of the great houses themselves were perhaps VIP seating for hundreds of elites. Downtown Chaco was a city, but it was also a sacred theater, part natural and part carefully constructed.

Chacoan monumental building traditions extended well beyond the canyon. Great houses, usually much smaller than those in the canyon but built with similar technologies and according to similar design canons, are found as far as 150 miles away. These sites are quite variable (see chapter 10), but the range of forms and masonry styles seen in so-called outliers is met or exceeded by architectural variation within Chaco Canyon great houses, which range from very large to rather small buildings. Roads, earthworks, and other major elements of Chacoan building appear throughout the region. Together, shared forms and details suggest a region-wide architectural tradition. Clearly, that tradition

found its most remarkable expression in Chaco Canyon itself, and it seems likely that Chacoan architecture outside the canyon was inspired by or referred back to Chaco Canyon. Architecturally, Chaco Canyon was the center of the larger region.

Alden Hayes and Tom Windes's discovery of a sophisticated line-of-sight communication network extends the built environment of Chaco Canyon to its region, perhaps to its very farthest corners (see chapter 11). This line-of-sight system, presumably operated with smoke or mirrors, paralleled the more famous Chacoan roads and ultimately may prove to be more important to understanding Chaco and its world. Strategic high points throughout the Chaco region feature large fire boxes and shrines that are visible from other, more distant high points where outlier great houses are situated. For example, Katy Freeman, a high school student, discovered that Chimney Rock Pueblo (see photo p. 89) was positioned to allow line-of-sight to Huérfano Mountain, in northern New Mexico. Huérfano Mountain (which has the remnants of many fire boxes and shrines) in turn has direct line-of-sight to Pueblo Alto. Presumably, messages could have been passed from Chimney Rock, at the northeastern edge of the Chacoan region, to downtown Chaco in a matter of minutes if people were manning the "repeater" station at Huérfano Mountain. The signaling system would have required careful management, staffing, and coordination. Its existence throws light on the position of Pueblo Alto, with its views to the north; Peñasco Blanco, with its views to the west; and probably most other Chaco Canyon great houses.

For Chacoan architecture, we must understand far more than masonry details and ground plans of individual great houses. This was a monumental tradition, designed and built on citywide and even regional scales. Its shape reflects social, political, and ceremonial dimensions. In concept and execution, Chaco dwarfed other Southwestern architecture, with the possible exceptions of the massive ceremonial complex at Aztec Ruins (which flourished in the twelfth and thirteenth centuries) and the great city of Paquimé (fourteenth and fifteenth centuries) far to the south.

Andrew Fowler, John Stein, Keith Kintigh, and others have shown that after construction ceased in

Figure 4.6. New Alto, above Chaco Canyon on the north side, is a late great house with a dominant view of the surrounding countryside.

Chaco Canyon about 1125, the great-house tradition survived for decades at sites throughout the old Chaco region. As I explained in my book *The Chaco Meridian* (Altamira Press, 1999), I believe Aztec and Paquimé were direct architectural heirs of Chaco. In any event, Chacoan architecture deeply influenced subsequent Pueblo building and history. Chaco great houses were, indeed, the first structures in what we today call "Pueblo style": terraced, multistory architecture. Modern Pueblo style replicates the forms of Chacoan buildings but probably not the social, political, and ceremonial complexities that shaped them.

Chacoan architecture was distinctive, but was Chaco unique? Like any other great tradition, Chaco had its particular history. But we cannot lose sight of its context: arable North America in Chaco's time was densely populated by monumental social-ceremonial centers, some smaller but most larger than Chaco. The Chacoans clearly knew the polities of Mexico far to the south; closer to home, however, were the numerous "chiefdoms" of the Mississippi Valley, with their huge ceremonial and political centers.

Cahokia, the largest Mississippian site and contemporary with Chaco, provides an interesting comparison. Located near St. Louis in the rich farmlands of the American Bottom, it includes as its main feature an earthen pyramid as large as the largest in Mexico. Scores of smaller "mounds" and monuments define a complex ceremonial cityscape that was comparable in spatial extent but larger in population than Chaco Canyon. No more than three thousand people lived at Chaco, in comparison with ten thousand or more at Cahokia.

Thus, Chacoan architecture was unique within the Southwest of its time, but it was comparable to the architecture of hundreds of other monumental centers of the eleventh and twelfth centuries in Mexico and North America. We rightly marvel at Chacoan building, but we should not be unduly surprised that Native Americans built large, monumental ceremonial-political centers in the ancient Southwest: such centers were present almost everywhere else that corn could be grown on Chaco's continent.

Of course most of those centers, such as Cahokia, were built in far better farming environments than

The massive Pueblo Bonito with the canyon cliffs rising behind.

Excavators at work at Pueblo Alto, late 1970s.

Pueblo Pintado great house east of central Chaco Canyon.

Chetro Ketl's tower kiva.

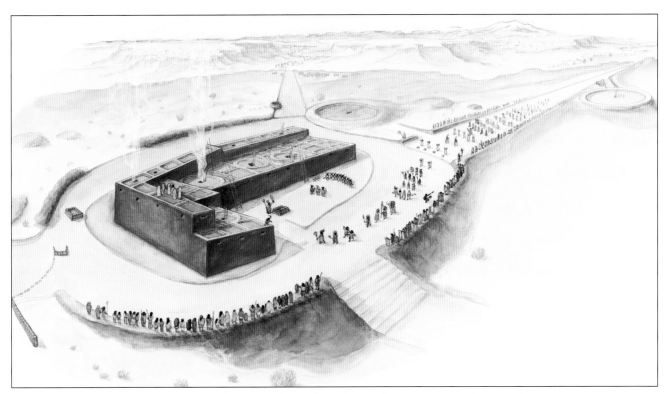

Artists' reconstruction of Kin Hocho'i outlying great house by Robert and Karen Turner. The scene depicts a procession passing between two great kivas along a wide roadway. Local folk gather on an earthen berm surrounding the Chacoan structure to watch dancers in the plaza.

Guadalupe Pueblo, an outlying great house southeast of Chaco Canyon. In the distance are the Rio Puerco and Cabezon Peak.

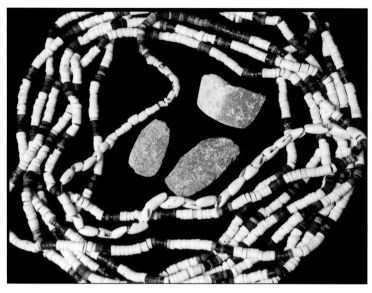

A fourteen-foot-long necklace of shell and stone beads, along with three pieces of turquoise, all from a wall niche in Chetro Ketl's great kiva.

Chaco corrugated jar (1075–1225) excavated from Kin Kletso.

Craft arts from Pueblo Bonito excavated by the Hyde Exploring Expedition of 1896–1899 and now in the American Museum of Natural History. Left: reconstructed turquoise-encrusted cylinder; center: deer bone spatula or scraper inlaid with jet and turquoise; right: McElmo Black-on-white pitcher.

A McElmo Black-on-white pottery canteen from Chetro Ketl.

Figure 4.7. Aztec West, a major Chacoan great house along the Animas River.

Chaco's. It is easier to imagine ten thousand people living and farming in the American Bottom and building Cahokia than to envision three thousand surviving at Chaco, much less producing sufficient corn, beans, and squash to support the building of great houses, platform mounds, roads, and other monuments.

Chaco was monumental. *Modestly* monumental —Chaco was not Cahokia. Still, it was far more than a valley full of pueblos. Chacoan architecture itself is our best and biggest clue that Chaco was actually a city, with a resident elite controlling a region. Great houses themselves represent stratified housing. They cost a lot to build per square foot of floor space, and their builders used superior materials and construction techniques. They were built to last. Whereas a small site might be abandoned or rebuilt every generation, Pueblo Bonito stood for nearly three centuries, and large sections of it still stand today. Great houses strongly suggest that their residents were of a different class from the people who lived in small houses, a fact born out by many other lines of evidence related in the chapters of this book.

Stephen H. Lekson is an associate professor of anthropology and curator of anthropology at the Museum of Natural History, University of Colorado, Boulder. He has conducted Chaco-related research since the mid-1970s and was a member of the Chaco Project. His books include *Great Pueblo Architecture of Chaco Canyon* and *The Chaco Meridian*.

Figure 5.1. Chaco Black-on-white jar, about 1050–1200, 14.5 inches in diameter by 14.5 inches high, found in a sand dune in Escavada Wash.

Artifacts in Chaco

Where They Came From and What They Mean

H. Wolcott Toll

It's a long drive from Skunk Springs in the Chuska Valley to Chaco Canyon. There's not much out there today. Imagine walking that distance—more than forty miles of sand and arroyos and mesas. Imagine carrying a wooden rack loaded with twenty or more clay pots, or being part of a team carrying a ponderosa pine roof beam across those miles. Ancestral Pueblo people undertook such treks thousands of times in the two and a half centuries during which Chaco Canyon's great houses were being built and used.

Looking around Chaco Canyon today, with its scarce trees and shrubs, it is easy to understand why builders there had to import roof beams from the surrounding mountains. But the canyon abounds in good clay sources for pottery making, so why did its people also use huge numbers of vessels made in faraway places? Why did they bring quantities of stone for cutting tools to Chaco when usable stone could be found close at hand? Probably every Chaco household was able to fill most of its own basic needs, but instead they acquired many items from other areas, sometimes at considerable distances. Why?

The answer is complicated, but exchanges of goods helped cement social relationships. Making a living in the semiarid Southwest was never easy, and in a year when the rains shortchanged farmers in one area, those in another might have been blessed with ample rainfall. For people whose storerooms were bare, having friends, trading partners, or even other houses in more fortunate places could be lifesaving. And for people throughout the region, gaining access to ceremonies conducted in Chaco's celebrated great houses might have been ample reward for their

products or labor. Taking part and bringing what you could required a long trip, but it also involved making new acquaintances, socializing with old friends, and collecting critical information on where resources were available.

To discover the ebb and flow of people in Chaco Canyon, archaeologists look to artifacts collected from sites there and attempt to identify where they were made. Knowing the geology of the area, researchers can recognize the sources of clays used to make pots and the sources of tempering materials—sand or bits of crushed rock, for example—that potters kneaded into their clay to prevent vessels from cracking during drying and firing. Similarly, geologists have mapped outcrops of certain kinds of stone, and these can be matched with artifacts made of the same stone.

Ringing the arid central San Juan Basin, in which Chaco Canyon lies, are the Chuska Mountains on the west, the Dutton Plateau and Mount Taylor on the south, the Jemez Mountains on the east, and the San Juan River, which drains several mountain ranges, on the north. These higher, wetter environments offer many natural resources, including the volcanic rock, timber, and fuel wood that are scarce in the basin itself. The Chuska Mountains are especially graced with resources, including ponderosa and fir forests, streams, trachyte—a distinctive tempering material— and high-quality Narbona Pass chert. Not surprisingly, many ancestral Puebloans lived in and around the Chuska Valley, which lies along the eastern flank of the mountains, throughout the occupation of Chaco Canyon. Both Narbona Pass chert and trachyte

Figure 5.2. A summer storm brews over the arid San Juan Basin between Chaco Canyon and the Chuska Mountains.

temper come from a small area in the mountains and are very distinctive, and the people used them intensively. Their frequent occurrence in Chaco Canyon sites repeatedly directs our attention to the Chuska Mountains and the residents of the Chuska Valley as we try to understand Chaco Canyon itself.

Every Pueblo household had a basic tool kit for daily use. It normally included pottery for cooking, serving, and storage; cutting tools (usually just broken pieces of stone with very sharp edges) and hammers for making other tools and fitting building stones; grinding stones for processing plant foods; and bone tools for sewing and basket making. In what follows, I summarize the sources of some of the items that households in Chaco used, in order to show how interdependent they were with their neighbors near and far. Then I attempt to put all the pieces back together in a look at Chaco's larger role in a vast network of social and economic connections.

Chaco's Pottery

Pottery is a mainstay for studying questions of exchange. At a minimum, each family owned gray pottery jars for cooking and storage and black-on-white painted bowls, ladles, and pitchers for serving

food—though any one family's full array of vessels was probably more varied and interesting than this brief list suggests. Even the unpainted, utilitarian gray pottery came in different shapes and sizes, and potters often textured the surfaces of these vessels in visually pleasing ways (see photo in color section).

The tempers and clays from which potters fashioned their gray wares reveal a surprising variety of sources for the pots found at Chaco Canyon. In most other parts of the Pueblo world in the late 1000s, people mostly used utility pottery made of local materials. In contrast, more than half the gray pottery in Chaco by that time came from the Chuska Valley, even though it lies some forty desolate miles from central Chaco Canyon. The sources of many other imported vessels are less easily or confidently identifiable, but archaeologists think that by the late 1000s, very little pottery was being made in Chaco Canyon. No potential firing locations are known, and all of the pottery-making tools have been excavated from structures dating before 1000 or even 900.

Why was so much utility pottery imported into Chaco Canyon? Surely one reason was that the large amounts of fuel needed for firing pottery were hard to come by in the canyon. In addition, some of the

Figure 5.3. Left to right: two Chuska Black-on-white bowls and a Cíbola White Ware bowl.

that even the trachyte-tempered Chuska white wares had different makers.

Chaco Canyon sites contain small quantities of two other kinds of pottery: red ware and polished, smudged brown ware. These wares point to other distant groups of people who either visited Chaco Canyon themselves or else interacted with Puebloans who lived closer to Chaco and who visited the canyon on occasion, bringing vessels with them. Most of the brown wares are bowls with lustrous black interiors; they resemble present-day black wares made in Santa Clara and San Ildefonso Pueblos. This pottery came from the Mogollon region of east-central Arizona and western New Mexico.

vessels might have contained food, and as we will see, social reasons were important, too. In any case, we can be sure that throughout the Puebloan world of the time, some people produced more pottery than others, and some households—or even villages—made little or no pottery. Although we have no evidence for factory-style production of pottery or other goods, the presence of so much nonlocal pottery in Chaco Canyon shows that even household specialists could produce pottery well beyond needs of the immediate locality.

As for black-on-white painted pottery, its potential sources were vast. Artisans had been manufacturing this accepted style throughout northern Arizona, southeastern Utah, southwestern Colorado, and most of New Mexico west of the Rio Grande since the 600s. Their decorative styles conformed to a well-defined set of designs and layouts, indicating that they were part of a regional culture, familiar with other potters' work and subscribing to a common set of beliefs. Chacoans imported black-on-white vessels from the Red Mesa Valley south of the canyon, from northeastern Arizona, from north of the San Juan River, and from the Chuska Valley, among other far-flung places. Differences in paint types show

The red wares, too, have been found mostly as bowls. Their finely painted oranges and deep reds form striking contrasts to the ubiquitous black-on-white decoration. From 700 to 1050 CE, Chacoans acquired most of their red ware vessels from people in southeastern Utah, north of the San Juan River. Indeed, this is the only sort of pottery from north of the San Juan that is at all common in Chaco sites. San Juan Red Ware production faded out in the 1000s, and in its stead, Chacoans began to trade for Kayenta orange and polychrome pottery made in northeastern Arizona and for White Mountain Red Ware from around Zuni in west-central New Mexico.

The accompanying graph illustrates the changing pace of ceramic importation to Chaco Canyon. Chaco Project archaeologists collected the majority of the pre-1040 pottery from habitation sites near Fajada Butte and most of the late-1000s samples from the parts of the Pueblo Alto great house they excavated. The latest periods are represented only by very small samples. The graph tells us that the

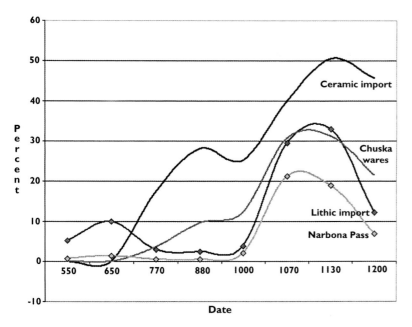

Figure 5.4. Percentages of materials imported to Chaco Project sites through time, showing Chuska ceramics and Narbona Pass chert as well as overall imports. Although the Chuskas were a major source of imports, some materials were brought into Chaco Canyon from other areas.

groups of people active in Chaco imported dramatically more pottery during the height of great-house construction, from 1030 to 1100, though the explosion of trade was grounded in a firm foundation of long-standing practices. Residents of the Chuska slopes were the principal—but far from the only—outside suppliers, especially of utility pottery.

The Importation of Stone

Any visitor to Chaco Canyon quickly becomes aware of its scarcity of fuel and water, but rock is hardly in short supply. Sandstone is everywhere, a ready source for the large grinding tools—chiefly metates (flat or troughed slabs) and manos (hand stones)—that the Chacoans used to prepare corn. Metates are large, heavy blocks of sandstone, and a great deal of human labor went into finding the right stone for the right purpose, transporting it to where it would be used, shaping it, and putting it in place. Presently, researchers have difficulty determining the sources of particular sandstones, and metate sources might someday surprise us. For now, however, archaeologists assume that Chacoans acquired their sandstone for heavy grinding tools

from as close by as possible, so long as it met the requirements for a good metate. The value of metates is demonstrated by the fact that though they were the largest, heaviest tools in the kit, their users almost always removed them and presumably took them along when they stopped using a room or left their home. Archaeologists often find metate rests and meal catchment basins, but it is rare for metates still to be in place. Given the ritual and social importance of grinding corn among the historic and contemporary Pueblo Indians, it is clear that more attention should be given to this subject.

Cutting tools, which people made by chipping rather than grinding, have different requirements. Rather than the large, abrasive stones suitable for grinding tools, cutting tools need to be made from stones that break with a sharp, durable edge and can be shaped into thin, predictable forms. For these purposes, makers used locally available cherts, petrified wood, chalcedonies, and quartzites. Finding usable pieces of such stone required knowledge and some searching and transport, but the supply was adequate and the distances were not great.

What is perhaps surprising is that although the people of Chaco could have filled all their needs for chipped stone tools with rock close at hand, they still imported a great deal of stone from distant sources. For example, they got obsidian, a volcanic rock, from people living in the Jemez Mountains to the east and around Mount Taylor to the south—both sites of ancient volcanism. Oddly, more obsidian was imported into Chaco Canyon in the early years (before 800 CE) and the later ones (after 1100) than during the main building period.

Links to other areas encircling the San Juan Basin are evident in the importing of yellow chert from the Zuni area and green chert from the Four Corners. During Chaco's period of greatest activity (1040–1110), its residents imported significant quantities of a distinctive pink chert from the Chuska area—Narbona Pass chert. It made up as much as 26 percent of the stone excavated at Pueblo Alto. Whereas obsidian, which came from at least as far away as Narbona Pass chert, is usually found at Chaco as finished tools such as projectile points, Narbona Pass chert, like the chipped-stone tool kit in general, was seldom shaped beyond rough flaking into expedient

Figure 5.5. Metates in place as they were found, Pueblo Bonito, 1896–1898.

Animal products, too, made up fundamental parts of both the tool kit and the diet. Unfortunately for archaeologists, we are not yet able to trace faunal sources through chemistry, and animals have the analytically inconvenient ability to move among environments and geological zones.

One change we do see in the animal bones excavated from Chaco sites is a greater proportion of deer bones during the 1000s. Both deer and pronghorn antelope live in and around the canyon today, but deer are more numerous and inhabit a wider range of environments. Although rabbits were always an important source of protein, people consumed increasing quantities of deer throughout the 1000s. Pronghorns became an insignificant part of the diet, probably because early hunters depleted the herds. Heavier reliance on deer, which favor woodland environments, conforms to the increased transport of pottery, chert, and timber from mountainous zones. Even if hunters continued to take some game closer to the canyon, the means for supply over longer distances were already in place.

cutting edges. This handsome stone probably had more than functional meaning. Its presence in Chaco sites reiterates the close Chaco-Chuska link we have already seen in pottery.

Plants and Animals

Pots and pieces of stone were not the only items acquired from outside the canyon. Some plant and animal products, too, came from elsewhere in the San Juan Basin and the highlands surrounding it. Although a few ponderosa pines grow today in isolated pockets near central Chaco, firs and spruce trees were absent from the canyon during ancestral Pueblo times. Bringing in tens of thousands of construction timbers from afar required enormous human effort.

When researchers look at the species of wood found in Chaco sites at different times, a clear pattern emerges. Trees that were harvested in later years came from higher elevations and therefore greater distances from the canyon. Exciting new chemical analyses are even allowing archaeologists to discover where the trees grew, and again our attention is directed to the Chuska Mountains and Mount Taylor. The same principles that are beginning to reveal where trees grew are being applied to corn (see sidebar). Very preliminary results again point to the Chuska Valley in the Newcomb area as a source for some cobs excavated from Pueblo Bonito. Testable samples of corn, however, are far fewer than testable samples of timber.

Exotic Items

More famous and eye-catching than utility pottery and unshaped pieces of chert are goods that reached Chaco Canyon from even greater distances. Some of these have been uncovered at Chaco sites in much greater abundance than anything found in other ancestral Pueblo sites of the time.

Turquoise is the most famous of the "exotics" and the one for which we have the best understanding of production and use. Archaeologists discovered most of Chaco's finished turquoise at Pueblo Bonito, where tens of thousands of pieces were cached or buried with the dead. Although turquoise probably came from a number of sources, an important one was the Cerrillos Hills, south of modern Santa Fe and east of the Rio Grande. Puebloan people mined turquoise in this area from at least as early as the 900s and on into historic times, and their products found their way across the entire Southwest.

Chaco's Corn
Where Was It Grown?
Linda S. Cordell

Maize, or corn, was the dietary staple of the ancestral Pueblo people of Chaco Canyon, as it was for Native Americans throughout the Southwest. Archaeologists differ about the potential for ancient agriculture in Chaco Canyon and how large a population it could have supported (see chapter 2). Two kinds of chemical analyses of excavated ancient corn—tests that measure the ratio of strontium 86 to strontium 87 and the ratios of some trace elements—reflect the chemistry of the water in the soil in which the corn was grown. Experiments with modern Native American corn and extensive testing of sites of known or potential ancient fields can, in theory, enable researchers to match ancient corn to places where it was grown.

A recent experiment in which six other researchers and I collaborated showed that ancient maize excavated from the oldest section of Pueblo Bonito was grown in fields fifty miles to the west, along Captain Tom Wash on the Chuska Mountain slopes. Six cobs dated between 850 CE and the mid-900s, and one dated between 1088 and 1150. Although we had a small sample of cobs, none matched the soil water chemistry of Chaco Canyon.

The analyses show that, in addition to utilitarian items such as pottery and chert and exotics such as turquoise and parrots, the people of Chaco also imported some of their basic food. Future studies of this kind on a larger scale may reveal the extent to which corn was transported to Chaco Canyon from distant growing areas and whether or not the Chacoans used the oversized rooms of the great houses for bulk storage. This, in turn, may shed more light on the network of social relationships among people living throughout the San Juan Basin and give us a key to understanding how related and interdependent the Chaco system really was.

Clear evidence exists that Chaco artisans themselves fashioned imported turquoise into ornaments. In some of the habitation, or "small," sites that dot the canyon, archaeologists have uncovered thousands of tiny fragments of turquoise along with tiny chert drills. Many small sites have turquoise waste amid their surface litter. Apparently, the people living in the small sites were making important artifacts that were later deposited in the great houses. Perhaps turquoise was their entrée to what went on at the great houses. Alternatively, perhaps the leaders of activities at the great houses were able to require it of the residents of small houses.

Two other noteworthy exotics at Chaco sites arrived from even farther away than turquoise. Copper bells probably were the products of artisans in what is now western Mexico, and scarlet macaws, with their spectacular feathers in rare and symbolically important colors, came from the tropics. Altogether, fewer than fifty bells have been found in Chacoan sites, and more than thirty of those came from Pueblo Bonito alone. The distribution of macaws is similar to that of the bells. Nevertheless, the two offer clear evidence of linkages between Chaco and people who lived quite differently from the ancestral Pueblos.

Archaeologists often mention copper bells, macaws, and turquoise as links to Mesoamerican cultures—birds and bells as imports and turquoise as an export. Evidence for knowledge from and about the complex societies to the south runs like a thread through the history of societies in the Chaco region, but what exactly was the nature of exchange between the two areas? Scholars have yet to establish that turquoise from the American Southwest appears in substantial quantities in Mesoamerican sites, so its status as a Chacoan export remains speculative. Finished turquoise objects have been found in Chaco Canyon as offerings in kiva pilasters dating to the 1000s, in great kiva niches, under slabs in Pueblo Bonito, and with burials in Pueblo Bonito. Together these finds suggest that turquoise was being removed from circulation in order to mark Chaco as a special place rather than being amassed for shipment to Mexico.

Copper bells and macaws, too, have been found concentrated in a few locations in Chaco sites, but

Figure 5.6. Guatemalans in recent times carrying heavy loads of pottery up a mountain road. This scene offers a clue to how pottery might once have been transported from the Chuska Mountains and other areas to Chaco Canyon.

they were unaccompanied by other southern symbols of status. It seems more likely that these exotic goods were neither items of exchange nor the possessions of imperialistic lords but emblems of Chacoans' connections to important and powerful, if distant, people and forces.

Social Cement

To a certain extent, archaeologists can only speculate about what kinds of social relationships existed among people living in and around Chaco Canyon. Yet we know that impressive quantities of goods changed hands between people of different areas, and we feel certain that these exchanges were important socially and economically. People living in Chaco had pragmatic, resource-based reasons for importing some items, but even in those cases the quantities seem too large, especially if, as many researchers think, the population of the canyon was quite small. Why is there so much? I believe the answer can best be addressed by asking another question: What was Chaco Canyon, and how did its social and economic system operate?

The concept that for me best expresses what Chaco Canyon was is a community of communities. By this I mean that Chacoan society embraced people who lived throughout the San Juan Basin and in the surrounding highlands, incorporating them into a social and religious system centered in the canyon's great houses. Throughout the Chaco region, settlements were organized into groups of habitations with associated public structures (see chapters 10 and 11). These communities, in turn, were linked to Chaco Canyon, which held public architecture for the larger region. The archaeologist Marcia Truell has commented on the great variety of ways people constructed small sites in Chaco Canyon, which she interprets as the result of building by people from different locations. Perhaps families who visited the canyon to work on great-house construction, to celebrate, and to interact maintained small-site residences there in addition to their homes in other places.

Indeed, the extent to which people moved around the region probably far exceeded anything we might have expected. Because so much pottery, stone, and lumber at Chaco originated in the Chuska

Mountains, I think it likely that many households had residences in both places, which they occupied at appropriate times in the agricultural and ritual cycles. But although the Chuska presence is especially clear in the archaeological record, we must remember that it also serves as a proxy for the involvement of other communities in other locations that are less distinctly visible in the record. The salience of the Chuska connection should not be allowed to eclipse the importance of other community ties.

I mentioned earlier that the reward participants received for providing goods to Chaco Canyon might have been access to its religion, ceremonies, and prestige. One thing that makes me suspect this is that whereas corridors along which materials flowed into the canyon are visible, flow outward is not. For example, Chuska pottery flowed into Chaco and stopped there; it did not continue to other areas. Roads in our culture are all about transport and travel, but in Chaco they were at least as much about symbolic connections between places.

Chaco society was above all scheduled and planned. People shared a sense of symmetry and order and a vision backward and forward through time on a scale unfamiliar to us. Within the strictures of an agricultural calendar, when communal events happened—events such as building projects, landscaping, and religious observances—was crucial. A deep subscription to the tenets of an encompassing ceremonial order that cross-cut many groups, both geographically and socially, was crucial to participation by a dispersed population that provided large bursts of labor and material. The fundamentals of this belief system were deeply rooted and became increasingly elaborated over time through incorporation of new groups and areas. This deep foundation was fertile ground for a hugely increased effort to expand the size and influence of Chacoan society during the eleventh century. Whether this effort was initiated for the general good or for personal gain, opportunities for manipulating people lay in the control of scheduling. Chaco's leaders apparently wanted the place to have even greater earthly and spiritual significance, and they had the personal prestige and charisma to make it happen. Theirs was a short run, but it had a long epilogue and many iterations in subsequent centuries.

Spread as they were over a vast region, participants in the Chaco idea embraced certain common ideas and beliefs that are reflected in the patterns of their material culture and built landscape. At the same time, there were regional variations in these cultural patterns and group allegiances that changed through time and space.

Chaco Canyon was a place permeated with meaning, embellished and elaborated to remarkable degrees through ritual. But whatever ideology or belief system lay behind the overarching community, its constituents also had to function at a material and subsistence level. Thus, the canyon was a place where inhabitants of the San Juan Basin made economic and social connections with their neighbors. Very likely these connections happened in the context of religious gatherings, which provided an effective means of mustering labor and transporting goods.

Part of what makes a place and time are its sources of joy. What made people happy in Chaco? I think it was things done and made well, things done right: ceremonies, buildings, pots, jewelry, work. Beauty. Rain. A great view. Connections. Full storerooms. An exciting game of chance or a race. Balance and symmetry.

Chaco was many things: A turning point. Awesome. Demanding. Windy. Hot. Cold. Dry. And we must never lose sight of this: Even in good times, it was never easy. In those circumstances, having friends and associates over a large area and keeping up the social conditions necessary to maintain those relationships were crucial to survival. The combination of material and symbolic exchange was solidified by widespread subscription to an impressive and coherent belief system. The system and the people and places participating in it changed regularly through time, and its fullest expression and extent may have been relatively brief, but it left a mark on the cultural landscape that survives to the present.

H. Wolcott Toll has spent most of his archaeological career working in the ancestral Pueblo area of Colorado and New Mexico. He excavated sites and analyzed pottery for the National Park Service's Chaco Project from 1976 through 1985; since then he has worked for the Office of Archaeological Studies of the Museum of New Mexico.

Yupköyvi

The Hopi Story of Chaco Canyon

Leigh J. Kuwanwisiwma

Aliksa'i. Listen, let us begin. From the four cardinal directions they came. The Hisatsinom, the ancestral Hopi, were certain that a place called Yupköyvi, "the place beyond the horizon," was their destination.

The appropriate signs were there. The great blue star called the Sakwasohu—the supernova of 1054—had appeared in the heavens. This portent told the migrating clans to end their journeys and await further signs. Many clans had indeed fulfilled their covenant with Masaw, the spiritual guardian of the earth. This covenant dictated that clans journey to the four corners of the present world, place their footprints, and await further directions.

Masaw's guidance told the old ones that they had to begin a convergence on Yupköyvi, the place known today as Chaco Canyon. It was a place where knowledge was to be shared and where the people would make final deliberations about their ultimate destination.

This is a part of their story.

Antsa Yaw Yanhaqam Hiniwti: Yes, This Is the Way It Happened

It is well known among observers of the Hopi people that they continue to hold onto their traditions amid enormous strain. Indeed, it is amazing that Hopi ceremonies and traditions still play such a key role in Hopi life, enabling Hopi clans to understand and respect their individual cultural histories.

Archaeological evidence from Pueblo Bonito, for example, illustrates the use of ceremonial wands similar to those used today among Hopi religious societies. Scientific correlation of Hopi traditions with practices at places such as the ancient villages of Chaco Canyon does not surprise the Hopi people.

How did the people of Yupköyvi come to be? This is our knowledge about them.

The beginning of the fourth way of life was one of simplicity. The Motisinom, the "first people," whom archaeologists call Basketmakers, were planting, hunting, and harvesting wild plant foods in and around the valleys of the Chaco region. Song and social interaction were the spiritual forces that bonded these people. Their lives centered on their subsistence tasks and care of their environment. Among the Hopi clans descended from these people are the Katsina, Badger, Gray Badger, Tobacco, and Cottontail Rabbit clans. Today these people play important roles in the winter and summer katsina ceremonies.

According to oral traditions, these early ancestral Hopis occupied a vast territory in which they cultivated corn and squash, hunted game, and gathered edible plants. Their lifeway required cooperation and reciprocity. Clan groups lived side by side and traded with one another. At appropriate times, they played competitive games, among which long-distance running was popular. They were excellent storytellers and song composers. On occasion the Motisinom held ceremonial dances that, although not elaborate or ritualistic, expressed contentment, happiness, and gratitude, especially in years of good harvest.

The first people of the Chacoan landscape were travelers and traders, too. They journeyed west to trade with the people of Koyongtupqa, or Canyon de Chelly, where the Eagle and Badger clans ruled supreme. To the south, they traveled to Tsipiya (Mount Taylor).

Figure 6.1. Motisinom (Basketmaker) pictographs in Atlatl Cave, Chaco Canyon.

Turning east, they visited their relatives along the Hopoqwvayu (Rio Grande), stopping to rest at the early villages of the Acomas and Laguna. To the southwest, the Motisinom made pilgrimages to the ancestral villages of the Zunis to trade for salt.

These early people were not free from environmental challenges. Drought was especially feared. Hopi recollections about the past speak of hardship and suffering. Hence, the people always practiced preparedness.

Hopis today have cultural teachings that reach back to these trying times. Visit any Hopi household and you will learn that it keeps stocks of traditional food crops such as corn that will enable its members to survive for a period of time. The stone granaries that are found in abundance throughout the Chacoan valleys attest to this necessary behavior, one still practiced by contemporary Hopi people.

In order to survive in a sometimes unpredictable environment, the Motisinom mastered adaptable technologies that assisted them in wisely using their sometimes limited natural resources. An understanding of weather patterns, for example, allowed farmers to devise planting strategies for the coming year.

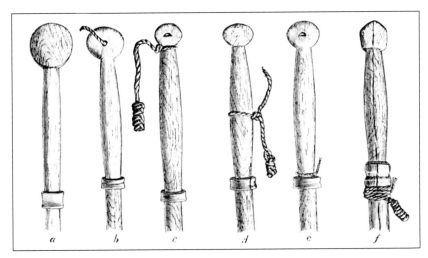

Figure 6.2. Ceremonial wands from Pueblo Bonito as illustrated in George Pepper's excavation report.

The Motisinom of Chaco also became astute observers of the cosmos. Their knowledge of astronomy enabled them to establish a calendar and ceremonial cycle and to keep track of mundane seasonal tasks.

All this, however, was early in the history of the Hisatsinom. This was the time of the Motisinom, the first people—the time before the great villages were built. Although their way of life seemed secure and the people content, events began to reshape the cultural setting the Motisinom had established.

Hopi clan traditions speak about other clan arrivals to the north, where many villages were being established. These clans had arrived from the west beyond the great canyon and from the southwest through Nuvatukyaovi, or the San Francisco Peaks. As the Hopi people say, "Yaw antsa naanani'vaqw öqiwta"—now from all directions they came. This emergence of more Hopi clans would forever change the cultural horizon of the first people.

But before we delve further into Hopi migration traditions, let us put them into the context of the modern-day Hopi perspective.

Itam Hapi Ngyamuy Amumi Toonawta: Our Clan Traditions Are Our Roots

Western perspectives about the modern Hopis are riddled with so many opinions that it is easy to understand why historians, anthropologists, ethnographers, fiction writers, and, more recently, "New Age" believers continue to argue over who is right. Few researchers have bothered to ask the Hopis who

they are. Those who did were treated with suspicion by Hopis and on some occasions deliberately given misleading information.

Only recently have researchers formalized their relationships with the very people they study. Formalizing means recognizing and accepting the Hopis' own research agendas and designs. Modern Hopi research is creative and does not arbitrarily dismiss science. Indeed, it seriously considers scientific findings and extracts information that corroborates Hopi traditional knowledge or is credible in terms of that knowledge. Although this may seem overselective, Hopis are not surprised that scientific conclusions complement their knowledge and verify cultural continuity between themselves and cultures thousands of years old.

Outside researchers sometimes casually misuse the terms "Hopi" and "Hopi tribe" without understanding their meanings. In 1998, the Hopi Cultural Preservation Office of the Hopi Tribe took the National Park Service to task when officials at Chaco Culture National Historical Park determined that twenty-one tribes, including the non-Puebloan Navajos, were "culturally affiliated" with human remains excavated from archaeological sites in the park. The key issue was not just flawed research by park personnel but the way they treated Pueblo people generically as if they were a single cultural group. The Park Service failed to accept the uniqueness of each tribe and conveniently chose to lump them all as descendants of the early Chacoan people. This dispute was compounded by the park's acceptance of the Navajos' political claim of affiliation to this prehistoric group.

I make this point about the Park Service because Western researchers also have tended to treat the particular clans they study as generically representing all Hopi people. Instead, outside researchers need to look at Hopis within their cultural context in order to understand their history through Hopi eyes.

Today there are thirty-four living Hopi clans and at least thirty additional extinct clans. Fundamental,

Figure 6.3. A Hopi bean field. The Hopi method of planting crops in sand dunes reflects farming methods used in Chaco Canyon in ancient times.

then, is to accept that there are sixty-four clan histories and, in many cases, specific clan religious beliefs and traditions. Ask any Hopi who he or she is, and you will receive the proud answer that the person belongs to a specific clan but is also a faithful practitioner of the Hopi philosophy of life.

This said, let us dive into the final chapter of Yupköyvi.

Itam Hapi Yaw Ang Kuktotani: We Have Been Instructed to Place Our Footprints

Hopi people consider themselves stewards of the earth. However, they did not just proclaim themselves such. As clan histories relate, clans earned the privilege of being spiritual caretakers. This privilege originated in the migration era of Hopi clans, an era based on a spiritual covenant with Masaw, guardian of the fourth era of life. Clans from the north, west, south, and east began to move into the Southwest. The Motisinom of Yupköyvi had visitors.

The strikingly visible archaeology we see in the Chaco area and at other well-known places such as Salapa (Mesa Verde) verifies the convergence of the migrating clans on these locations. The physical evidence reinforces Hopi traditional knowledge. The covenant with Masaw charged the Hisatsinom

to travel to the four cardinal directions, place their footprints, and await signs. Slowly, over perhaps two millennia or more, the Southwest became a mixture of different Hopi and other Puebloan clans and moieties that were embarking on deliberate journeys. Facing environmental hardships, the clans slowly placed their evidence to fulfill Masaw's spiritual pact. Today, the footprints of Hopi clans are defined as ruins, sacred springs, burials, landscapes, migration passages, artifacts, petroglyphs, and trading routes and trails.

To understand and express their history, Hopis rely on traditional knowledge and tangible practices such as song and ritual. For example, the appearance of the supernova of 1054—which, according to astronomers at the University of Arizona, was brightly visible for up to forty-five days—is today represented by the Blue Star Katsina, who routinely appears in the mixed Katsina dance. According to Hopi oral literature, this "blue star" was the supernatural sign to the Hisatsinom to end their migration and begin to converge on certain sites, including Yupköyvi (Chaco), Salapa (Mesa Verde), Hoo'ovi (Aztec Ruins), Kawestima (Navajo National Monument), Homolovi (the Winslow area), and Pasiwovi (Eldon Ruins, near Flagstaff).

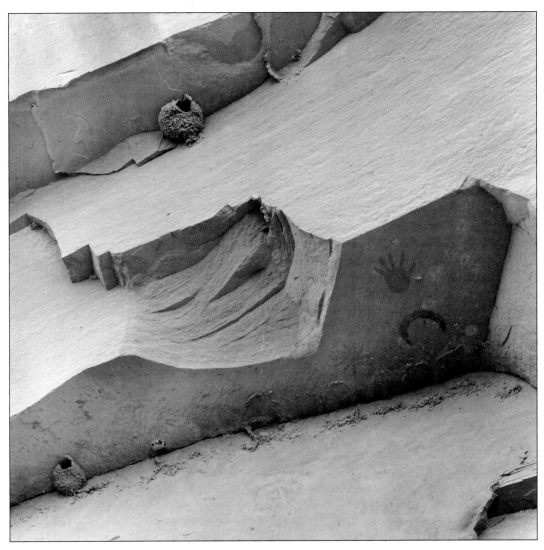

Figure 6.4. Pictographs near Peñasco Blanco in Chaco Canyon that may represent the supernova of 1054.

Thus Yupköyvi became a gathering place for clans from local areas as well as clans who had stopped at what might be described as "staging areas" some distances away. Among the initial clans to settle in the Chaco landscape were the Parrot and Katsina clans. Later, the Eagle, Sparrowhawk, Tobacco, Cottontail, Rabbitbrush, and Bamboo clans arrived. Carefully they were given places in which to establish their villages. According to tradition, this took time. Initial settlers became the ruling clans, which established order for the religious cycle as well as social responsibilities.

Together they contemplated their future. They shared their migration knowledge, spoke of the hardships they had endured, and cried out of sadness and joy. They learned to understand each other, even though they spoke different languages. Certain clans agreed that they must now prepare for the final journey to a place called Tuuwanasavi, the "earth center," which to the Hopis is their present home on the First, Second, and Third Mesas. Tuuwanasavi would be their final destination and their final home with Masaw.

But in order to be received and accepted by Masaw at Tuuwanasavi, they had to offer him something in return. This would be their respective bodies of clan and religious knowledge. This knowledge had to be complete and pure, for it was what each clan would ask Masaw to receive so that the clan could finally become Hopisinom—people of Hopi.

So each clan was allowed to establish itself at Yupköyvi. Each clan chose a matriarch and patriarch

Figure 6.5. Ancestral Pueblo petroglyphs in Chaco Canyon.

to lead it. The group collected its clan knowledge and incorporated it into its own ceremony. Then the clans announced that they would share their ceremonies publicly. Some clans were allowed to construct ceremonial kivas, where the elders guided their followers.

Finally, clan members performed their ceremonies. Some were elaborate, others simpler. All were performed and witnessed with the highest reverence.

All the ceremonies were for the good of the people—for good harvests, rain, and the perpetuation of life. This went on for many years as more clans arrived.

As time went on, the Hisatsinom of the Chaco area made contact with people of other great villages and established new trading routes. On one occasion the Bow clan of Hoo'ovi (Aztec Ruins) was beckoned to perform its great Salako (Shalako) ceremony.

Figure 6.6. Interior of the great kiva at Aztec Ruins as reconstructed by the National Park Service.

Figure 6.7. Casa Rinconada.

The clan leaders consented. Anticipation rose, for the reputation of the ceremony was well known. Together with the Bamboo and Greasewood clans, the Bow clan began its ceremonial preparations. This took years, they say. Finally, the trip to Yupköyvi happened. It was indeed a great sight as the Salako danced in the plaza. It rained.

The Bow clan members stayed at Yupköyvi for a long time, performing their dance four times every sixteen years. Then they returned to Hoo'ovi, from where they carried the ceremony to Awatovi and later to Orayvi. The many kivas at Pueblo Bonito are seen by Hopis as Salako kivas, because every time the ceremony was performed, a kiva "home" had to be constructed for it. Since the great Hopi Salako ceremony was fully resurrected at Hoo'ovi, the great kiva at Aztec is known to the Bow, Bamboo, and Greasewood clans as the Salak'ki, the "home of the Salako."

Another important ceremonial site in Chaco Canyon is the kiva known as Casa Rinconada. Its original purpose was as a site for the performance of the Hopi Lakon (basket) ceremony, under the ceremonial sponsorship of the Parrot clan.

Thus was life at Yupköyvi, until slowly the clans left for different places. The Hopi mesas were one destination. Other clans went to Halona, today's Zuni. Still others went to Zia, Acoma, and Laguna. Some chose to stay for a while longer, until they, too, left.

Yupköyvi had served its purpose, and now it was proper to lay it to rest.

For the many descendants of the Hopi clans that once lived in and around Yupköyvi, it will forever be their mother village. It is perhaps a distant, mysterious place beyond the horizon, but it is a place that lives in their hearts.

Pay yuk pölö. This is the end of the story.

Leigh J. Kuwanwisiwma, director of the Hopi Cultural Preservation Office, is a member of the Hopi Tribe, the Third Mesa village of Bacavi, and the Greasewood clan. He is a trustee of the Museum of Northern Arizona and serves on the Tribal Advisory Board of the Arizona State Museum. His personal interests include research into Hopi history, Hopi language preservation, and traditional Hopi farming.

Figure 7.1. Storm over Chaco Canyon.

A Pueblo Woman's Perspective on Chaco Canyon

Rina Swentzell

Fajada Butte showed itself in the misty distance as I made the last turn on the dirt road into the canyon. It was a late February day, and I wasn't feeling well. I had a cold, a sore throat that I was trying to ignore, and a heartache from family difficulties. Park rangers Russ and Tracy, who live in Chaco, graciously welcomed me into their living room—and there was Fajada Butte again. I could have stayed sitting on their couch and slowly fallen asleep with that butte in full view. But I also wanted to go to Pueblo Bonito and Chetro Ketl. We walked through those places with amazement at the dedication of work, degree of skill, and artistry of the classic Chacoans. As we talked, we had more questions than answers about why a wall appeared here or a pillar there. Dusk came quickly.

Snow, rain, and hail were my companions during the next day's walk to Peñasco Blanco. Gusty winds would precede the gifts of the clouds that loomed over the canyon walls. The orange-buff walls in unimaginable forms stood towering and threatening like strict guardians of the place. The sky changed unceasingly. The sun would shine for a bare minute or two between the fast-moving clouds. Then, late in the afternoon, an intense silence fell. I was stunned. There were no crows cawing, no twittering of smaller birds, no wind sounds. I stood amazed, feeling a depth of stillness that was beyond any other experience. I was startled by something small that bounced off the side of my head. Then another one hit my shoulder. Soon, small ice pebbles gave the sandstone pillars caps of white. The world was transformed.

The next day, as another park ranger and I looked at pictographs behind Wijiji, we talked about movement and change within the physical and cultural canyon. Through the talk of sites, solar orientation, and beauty of place, something happened—I touched another soul. This was not another Indian person who might predictably respond to the place as special because it was part of his ancestry. This was another human who responded with care and respect for the place because that was what his soul knew to do. I left Chaco that afternoon without a cold, without the sore throat, and with a lighter heart. I felt grateful for having once again experienced the beauty, mystery, and endurance of the place. I thought about the people who live in Chaco today and how they are part of the historical continuum of the canyon, which has endured waves of people coming and going, struggling, singing, surviving.

I was about twenty-eight when I first walked in Chaco Canyon. At Santa Clara Pueblo, where I grew up, we did not hear specifically about Chaco, but we knew that there were places throughout the land where "those gone on before us" had lived. In general, Pueblo people easily identify with any and all of those places, because making distinctions about who actually lived where and for how long is not the way we think. We dwell more on connections and know that even if the Hopis or the Zunis claim direct ancestry from the prehistoric Chaco people, we are all related through our common belief that we came out of the same earth. Our sense of the past is mythological, and our identity is ultimately

Figure 7.2. Fajada Butte.

For me, they represented a desire to control human and natural resources. They were not about the Pueblo belief in the capability of everyone, including children, to participate in daily activities, such that the process is more important than the end product. The Chaco great houses projected a different sensibility. The finished product was very important. Skill and specialization were needed to do the fine stonework and lay the sharp-edged walls. I concluded that the structures had been built by men in the prime of life with a vision of something beyond daily life and the present moment. These were men who embraced a social-political-religious hierarchy and envisioned control and power over place, resources, and people.

The caches of clay jars found in Pueblo Bonito also made me suspicious of the possible exploitation of women by such a hierarchy of men in control, who determined what and how much was made. I wondered whether the society had shifted in focus so that the process of making pottery for daily use, which nurtures relationships with the earth and other people, had been transformed to create objects for economic production and religious or political power.

When I left the canyon those thirty-some years ago, I was convinced that people from the south, from central Mexico, had built those great houses with the labor of the "locals." Later, I read that some archaeologists also suspected that people from Mesoamerica had influenced the way of building and the construction of roads and had encouraged intense ritualism, possibly for social control, during the classic Chaco period. How strange, though, that influence by however small or large an outside group could affect every aspect of living for hundreds of years in a large region within and around Chaco Canyon.

But when I think of modern Pueblo people, I know that newcomers are always welcome in our homes. Even people with different ways of doing things are tolerated, housed, and fed. It seems possible, then, that a group could have come through with the appropriate stories, songs, and dramas to

dependent on knowing that we humans are but one group of the earth's progeny. So when I first visited Chaco, the feeling of connection with the place was there—yet it was also puzzling, because it was different from being in Bandelier, Puye, or even Mesa Verde. The Chaco villages were grand, the rooms extra tall, and the walls massive and straight-edged.

Even then, my response to the canyon was that some sensibility other than my Pueblo ancestors had worked on the Chaco great houses. There were the familiar elements such as the *nansipu* (the symbolic opening into the underworlds), kivas, plazas, and earth materials, but they were overlain by a strictness and precision of design and execution that was unfamiliar, not just to me but in other sites of the Southwest. It was clear that the purpose of these great villages was not to restate their oneness with the earth but to show the power and specialness of humans.

Figure 7.3. A **nansipu** in Chetro Ketl's great kiva.

Figure 7.4. Chetro Ketl's colonnade, which faces the plaza, shows possible Mesoamerican influences in Chaco Canyon architecture. Note the fine stonework and sharp-edged walls.

north occupied some of the built sites and constructed others. Groups possibly from the Four Corners area came into the canyon, dressed the building stones differently, and made distinctive pottery but continued building smaller houses situated similarly to the great Chaco houses. These people from the north, if they came from there, would certainly have had contact with classic Chaco people, for there were also Chacoan great houses in the Mesa Verde and McElmo Canyon areas. Related groups of Chaco people could have gone north and returned into the Chaco Canyon area as a response to climate and social, political, or religious changes. The fact is, we don't know.

What we do know is that waves of people came and went from the canyon, as they did throughout the Southwest. Our present-day Pueblo belief system seems applicable here. It tells us that because we now dwell in the fourth world, where we know not only the stable earth but also the movement of the sun, moon, stars, and clouds, we know that movement is a desirable part of living. The climate and other factors might have encouraged movement, but movement might simply have been the way it was supposed to be in the minds of the people. And for whatever reason, movement certainly was chosen over remaining in the very permanent and stable great houses of Chaco.

Further, our Pueblo beliefs tell us that stability and movement are in cyclical relationship, such that one will surely follow the other. And so it is with the earth and the canyon. Change is certainly a part of their lives. As Chaco Wash changes its course and depth, the walls of the canyon peel off and tumble onto the canyon floor. The flora on the canyon floor changes, depending on animals and water. The canyon, because of its longer-than-human life span and its personality, has welcomed and expelled

convince the canyon residents that they could have greater control over resources and their lives if they did things differently. It seems, however, not to have been a one-way exchange, because many of the features from the old villages, such as kivas, nansipus, south orientation, and knowledge of resources, were continued in the great houses.

On another visit, I learned that after most of the classic Chaco people left the canyon, others from the

Figure 7.5. A School of American Research excavation crew at work in the great kiva of Chetro Ketl in the 1930s. The Navajo crew is using a winch and a mining car to remove fill.

many different groups of people. Ancestral Pueblo people, being sensitive to the way places feel, might have moved in response to the moods of the canyon.

It is interesting that the canyon rested from human presence for some years after the 1200s and into the time when the Navajos came during the early 1700s. Navajos are immensely resourceful people who thrive in the starkness of the Four Corners area, not in communities but in separate nuclear or extended family hogans. They have lived around the old village ruins and classic Chaco great houses, but they looked only from a distance with respect—and fear. They were not like the people from the north during the late 1200s who occupied the abandoned great-house structures. Nor were they like the nineteenth-century non-Indian treasure and adventure seekers who came into Chaco Canyon, disturbing the natural process of decay and return into the earth.

Again, a new human sensibility had arrived in Chaco. These were non-Native people who had a highly developed sense of the individual self, a need for power, and a hunger for adventure, things, and knowledge. They dug up Chaco's great houses, especially, and in some cases built them up again. Alongside archaeologists' claim to want to understand human history was their towing away of artifacts to faraway museums and even to personal collections. Parts of Chaco were dug, sifted, and scattered until other archaeologists, leaning toward preservation, succeeded in 1907 in having Chaco designated a national monument.

As preservationists prevailed, Chaco, as a place, changed again. Today, it feels different even from the way it felt those thirty-some years ago when I first walked there. It is more like a museum, where Don't Touch and Don't Enter are commonly posted signs. Sacredness is scarce in our modern world, and so protection of special places is necessary. And because a sense of sacredness is foreign, all possible information or knowledge is pulled out of the ground and the people. Everything and everybody is at the disposal of every other. Things are at the disposal of whoever gets there first. The entire West was claimed with that attitude. Richard Wetherill even took temporary ownership of Pueblo Bonito and Chetro Ketl as part of his homestead claim in the late 1800s.

Granting that every group has its issues, as I sit at home thinking about Chaco and the entire prehistoric Southwest, I know that people of European-American sensibilities are doing a lot of stereotyping today of that most glamorous classic Chaco period. A long-standing stereotype has been that the ancestral Pueblo people were passive, peaceful, and harmonious. That stereotype, however, is being challenged by some recent research that has received much publicity. Cannibalism and warfare are becoming common themes for a few archaeologists who are thinking about those times and claiming that everybody is really, after all, just like them and should be judged by their standards. Christy G. Turner and others show marks on human bones from the classic Chaco period that supposedly are definite signs of people's cutting up and cooking other humans. I believe there were times in the Southwest when cannibalism was necessary. As a child, I heard stories of historic Pueblo people's resorting to eating other people during times of extreme stress. And from our Pueblo point of view, why not? We eat deer, rabbits, and squirrels, and if humans are really only one of the earth's progeny, then why not other people—if it were necessary, as necessary as it is to eat a rabbit? To sensationalize necessary cannibalism is for people who believe humans are so special that human meat is unacceptable. It is for people who value human life above all other and assume that we are above and beyond the rest of the food chain.

As for warfare, any group of people experiences tensions and conflict, and conflict in the prehistoric Southwest is quite evident. Before people left the Four Corners area, archaeological reports show instances in which people were hit over the head and thrown into kivas, which might then have been set on fire. No signs of regional warfare, however, have come to light. I doubt that they will, because as societies struggle with errant behavior among individuals or groups, certain principles still guide the overall conduct of the majority. I believe that people of the classic Chaco era struggled with what was appropriate behavior. Although we suspect that Mesoamerican influences were felt in the region during that period, they vied with the values of an older and more enduring continuum that was native to the Southwest and served as a directive for most of the people. I believe that this directive of respect and care

for the earth and others, including plants and other animals, guided the people as they moved into areas outside the Four Corners and Chaco regions. It was a complex situation, with people trying to define and uphold appropriate behavior even though our human condition does include jealousy, envy, and hate. But stereotyping unnecessarily simplifies.

Drought and subsequent tensions have been part of the life story of Chaco Canyon. I wonder what we will do if the drought we are presently experiencing in the Southwest, as I write in 2003, were to last another fifteen years, especially if we could not depend on food coming from California and Mexico. Most of us, including Pueblo people, no longer have the skills to gather and grow our own food, even during normal times. I feel that the sensibility that came in during the 1800s is deeply within us. It claims that humans are superior to all other life forms and that our peculiar individual or group perceptions are the true and right ones.

What I ultimately learn from Chaco is that we swirl within great cyclical relationships. Chaco's starkness of landscape clarifies the necessary interdependence of humans with the clouds, the rabbits, and the rocks. Chaco challenges us to bend and touch the earth, to reach and touch the clouds, to touch other people so that our ideas of who they are or who we are can shift or be transformed because of our mutual touching. I wonder, can we flow with the transformation of the universe so that we can be part of the beauty and mystery of life, as Chaco has done over these centuries of human contact?

Rina Swentzell grew up in Santa Clara Pueblo and now lives in Santa Fe. She has a master's degree in architecture and a Ph.D. in American studies from the University of New Mexico. She has worked as a teacher, writer, and consultant for educational and architectural institutions. Her primary focus is her family, especially her twelve grandchildren.

Figure 8.1. Incised petroglyph of Navajo *ye'ii* (god) figure, Chaco Canyon.

eight

Tsé Bíyah 'Anii'áhí

Chaco Canyon and Its Place in Navajo History

Richard M. Begay

The use of oral history, whether from Navajo people or other Indian tribes, can bring us much closer to understanding Chaco Canyon. Traditional knowledge is a valid source of information in interpreting the canyon's development. The deeper we dig into the multiple layers of the Chacoan world, the more we begin to see and understand that Chaco was not a homogeneous culture, and we are bound to explore all available sources of information in order to understand it.

No one today can explain what really happened at Chaco Canyon. But judging from Navajo oral history, or *hane'*, we have an idea of what happened: the society was unable to overcome the ecological, economic, and social pressures of the day. Archaeologists, ethnologists, and others have spent countless hours digging, asking, writing, and contemplating how and why Chaco culture was developed, functioned, and then collapsed. Navajo people, like other Native peoples, rehash their histories and discuss among themselves what happened, what might have happened, and, more importantly, why it must not happen again. I would even guess that many Chacoans (who knows how they identified themselves?) did not know exactly what caused the breakdown of their Chacoan world. We are all curious about what happened. Our stories and our studies provide only a narrow context in which to frame our questions and a meager frame of reference for the Chaco culture. After more than a century of study, we still cannot comprehend all the complexities of the Chacoan world. The Navajo versions of what happened at Chaco can shed light on the development of Chaco and the Navajo people.

Hatáál Baa Hane': Navajo Ceremonial Stories

Chaco Canyon, its many outliers, and their inhabitants figure prominently in many Navajo ceremonies, including Atsájí (Eagle Way), Hoozhónee (Beauty Way), Mą'iijí (Coyote Way), Na'at'oyee (Shooting Way), Nílch'ijí (Wind Way), Tóee (Water Way), and Yoo'ee (Bead Way). The sites also figure in numerous miscellaneous ceremonial stories. The songs, stories, sandpaintings, and histories of these ceremonies directly reference places throughout Chaco Canyon, many of the outliers, and the people who lived in these places.

The best-known Navajo account of Chaco Canyon and the demise of Chaco culture centers on Nááhwíiłbįįhí, the Gambler (more correctly translated as "winner of people"). Nááhwíiłbįįhí came from a faraway place, south of the canyon. As he learned about the people in the Chaco environs, he began to manipulate them. He consolidated the population by moving them into the canyon, and under his influence they began to build the great structures whose remains we see today. Eventually he enslaved the people, and his orders became more severe and exacting. The accounts tell of his dissatisfaction with the architecture, the masonry style, and the sources of raw materials. He wanted finer architectural details and still more buildings to attribute to his magnificence. He is known to have lived at Pueblo Alto (Nááhwíiłbįįhí Bíkin, Gambler's House) and at other places throughout the canyon.

Through Navajo oral traditions, we know that hundreds, if not thousands, of people labored to build the structures we see today. Chaco was also a center of economic and social activity. At Pueblo Bonito, one could trade for anything: pottery, all types of food, clothing, ceremonial items, turquoise. The oral histories also tell us that the canyon was a place of many vices. It was the place for prostitution, sexual deviancy, and incest. Gambling was a common pastime; indeed, it was through gambling that Náahwíiłbįįhí was able to enslave the people. He was a preeminent gambler, and in the end each challenger had nothing left but himself or herself to wager. Thus, slowly, all challengers and their families became spoils of gambling and pawns of the Gambler. Náahwíiłbįįhí also used his slaves to gamble. For these reasons, the development of a place like Chaco Canyon must not happen again.

Náahwíiłbįįhí became so powerful that people feared he would begin to exercise control over the elements—rain, light (sun), and water—and they began to plot his downfall. As is recounted in Navajo history, the people, with the assistance of the Holy People, molded a young man who would become known as the Challenger to compete with Náahwíiłbįįhí. In the end, Náahwíiłbįįhí was defeated at his own games of chance and was forever banished. But before he was flung into the universe, he predicted that his children would one day return.

We know little about Náahwíiłbįįhí. We don't know exactly where he came from; we don't really know whether his children have returned. We know a little bit about the games of chance that he and the people engaged in, but beyond this general knowledge, we don't know how the game tools were constructed, what the rules were, and so forth. We don't even know what tools his slaves employed to build the great structures. Navajo traditions do tell us, however, that when Chaco culture collapsed, the former Chacoans moved on, some eventually becoming part of the modern-day Pueblo Indians (such as those at Zuni and the Rio Grande pueblos), and others becoming Navajos. Although many of the details are lacking, it is clear that Navajo ceremonial histories can enlighten us about the development and collapse of Chaco Canyon.

The Forming of Navajo People

Another way Navajo oral tradition can help us understand Chaco culture is through the clan origin stories of the Navajo people. These stories tell us that many of the people who inhabited the sites of Chaco Canyon and its associated network of sites throughout the Colorado Plateau became the progenitors of certain Navajo clans. (Clans are groups of people who share a common lineage from a place or one or more ancestors; for Navajos, descent is traced through women.) One of the largest clans, the Kin yaa'áanii (Towering House People), has roots in the Chacoan network, specifically at Kin yaa'á (Kin Ya'a Ruin), the outlier east of Crownpoint, New Mexico. The Kin yaa'áanii, like virtually all other Navajo clans, is divided into several subclans, among them the Dootł'izhii Dine'é (Turquoise People) Kin yaa'áanii and the Ţązhii Dine'é (Turkey People) Kin yaa'áanii.

Figure 8.2. Ruins of Kin Ya'a.

According to Navajo tradition, Ta̧zhii Dine'é or some variation of it existed in Chacoan society, and the Ta̧zhii Dine'é Kin yaa'áanii are the progeny of this much older clan. All Kin yaa'áanii, regardless of sub-clan affiliation, consider other clan members to be their kin and address each other as such. Therefore, all Kin yaa'áanii are at least indirectly related to some of the builders of the Chacoan culture.

According to the earliest version of the origins of Navajo clans, Kin yaa'áanii was one of the Four Original Navajo Clans, who are direct descendants of Asdzą́ą́ Nádleehé (Changing Woman). Changing Woman is the mother of all Navajo people and fig-ures prominently in many Navajo ceremonials. In brief, after the Holy People emerged into this world, they created the world as it is today. They formed the mountains and streams, and they put plants and rocks into place. But monsters and demons that inhabited this earth preyed on the people, and in order to destroy them, Changing Woman emerged. She gave birth to the Twins, Naayéé' Neizghání (Monster Slayer) and Tóbájíshchíní (Born for Water), who rid the earth of these afflictions and later became Holy Beings. Their mother continued to live with the people, however, until she decided to leave Navajoland and live in the western ocean (the Pacific Ocean), Tónteel. As she left she jour-neyed throughout the land and visited the people.

After a number of years, perhaps a generation or two after her departure, the people missed her, and some of them decided to visit her. After many days of travel, they finally found her on an island off the coast of what is now California. The people lived with her for several years before she decided they must return to Navajoland. Before they departed, she created four new groups of people, later to become known as the Four Original Clans, and among them was the Kin yaa'áanii. In other versions of the story, a member of the Kin yaa'áanii was among the travelers to the west-ern ocean, suggesting that Chaco Canyon was occu-pied during the time Changing Woman was living in Navajoland. The Kin yaa'áanii created by Changing Woman is possibly the subclan known as Hashch'éé Yáłti' Hayoołkááł (Talking God Dawn) Kin yaa'áanii. The members of this subclan consider themselves to be direct descendants of Changing Woman.

After the creation of the four clans, the people returned to Navajoland, encountering on their jour-ney enemies and relatives alike. Once within the area encompassed by the present-day Navajo Nation, the group traveled to visit their families and friends who had stayed behind. According to many versions of this trek, the people made a special trip to Chaco Canyon and some of its outliers, such as Kin Ya'a, to visit relatives.

Hashch'éé Yáłti' (Talking God) is said to inhabit large archaeological sites such as those found at Chaco Canyon and Mesa Verde, and perhaps the early members of Hashch'éé Yáłti' Hayoołkááł Kin yaa'áanii assumed the name after they had left these places and become Navajos as we know them today. If that is the case, there may be further divisions of this subclan that reflect their origins at Chaco Canyon

Figure 8.3. Archaeological crew members clear walls in the north roomblock of Pueblo Alto in about August 1976. Pictured are Jackson Begay, Wallace Castillo, Bruce Yazzi, Eddie Garcia, Victor Kee, Herman Etcitty, and Cory Breternitz.

and elsewhere, and those clans may be found in modern-day pueblos. Regardless of the various origins of the subclans, the Kin yaa'áanii among the Navajos attest to the prominence of Chacoan peoples in the development of the Navajo people.

The Historic Presence of Navajos in Chaco Canyon

Even modern Navajo people have a long history in Chaco Canyon. Some Navajos who live in the surrounding area assisted in the excavation of many of the Chacoan sites. Many of these workers considered the Chaco culture to be a part of their cultural heritage. The early Euro-American explorers, however, focused their attention on the pre-columbian sites and cultural material; only recently has the Navajo history of these places been recorded ethnographically.

Again, according to Navajo history, after the collapse of Chaco some of its inhabitants joined with Navajo groups, who by that time were living in hogans. Later Navajo people acquired sheep and began to live much differently from the people who built the Chaco culture. Archaeologists and others categorize Navajo sites as ethnically distinct from those of the *anaasází* (Navajo for "surrounding ancestral relatives" or "ancestral enemies") of Chaco Canyon, typically ignoring the remains of the former. That modern Navajo material culture looks different from Chaco material culture led anthropologists and archaeologists to assume they could learn nothing about the Chacoan people from Navajo history and ceremonies.

Historical and archaeological records show that Navajo people have resided in and around Chaco Canyon for centuries; indeed, Navajo people still live just outside the park boundaries. Navajo people have great respect for the Chacoan landscape. Other Navajo people live in the vicinity of other places associated with Chaco culture, in Navajo communities such as Coyote Canyon, Newcomb, and Tohatchi. In Chaco Canyon one can see the remains of Navajo life and culture off the beaten path. Rock art drawn by Navajos, depicting ceremonies, livestock and other animals, everyday life, and social events, decorates cliffs and boulders throughout the canyon. Hogan rings, corrals, and other vestiges of Navajo material culture dot the landscape in and around Chaco Canyon.

Although residence in the park today is restricted to park employees, Navajo people continue to use the canyon's resources. For example, they collect plants in the park for medicinal, ceremonial, and subsistence uses, as well as minerals for daily and ceremonial use. In addition, there are many places of sacred significance to Navajos throughout the canyon. Although the entire canyon may be considered sacred, a few places are especially respected, among them Tsé Diyilí (Fajada Butte), Tsé Bíyah 'Anii'áhí (Pueblo Bonito, also the general name for Chaco Canyon), and Nááhwíiłbįįhí Bíkin (Pueblo Alto). Furthermore, many Navajo names for Chacoan archaeological sites are incorporated into the interpretive literature distributed by the National Park Service, including Kin Kletso (Kin Łitsooí, Yellow House), Kin Bineola (Kin Bínaayol, House Encircled by Wind), and Shabik'eshchee Village (Shá Bik'e'eshchí, Sun Engraved on It).

Most pre-columbian archaeological sites can be sources of spiritual, sacred power. It is the mystery as much as our knowledge of Chacoan culture that makes these places, and the Chacoan people, essential to Navajo ceremonial

Figure 8.4. Navajo sweat lodge on Chacra Mesa.

Figure 8.5. Leo Chiquito, Chaco stabilization crew, 2003.

Lessons Learned from Navajo History

Oral history, hane', guides Navajos' understanding of the past, regardless of whether anthropologists and archaeologists find it informative. Nevertheless, the stories also suggest some answers to questions posed by archaeologists and anthropologists about Chacoan culture history. For example, perhaps Chaco was built by people under the influence of a single "person"—possibly an elite group personified by Nááhwíilbįįhí. Chaco was a regional trade and ceremonial center organized by an elite, and ceremonialism at Chaco might have included contests between the elites and outsiders from the surrounding region, possibly with a political outcome (losers became slaves or tribute payers). The stories also suggest that ceremonialism at Chaco included procedures for controlling great forces of nature—climate, precipitation, and celestial bodies. The people of Chaco eventually got rid of the elites through ceremonial competition. After the Chaco system fell apart, some residents who survived the Gambler period later joined with Navajos who lived in hogans around Chaco Canyon, and their descendants continue to occupy the Chaco region.

traditions and origins. Offerings are made at these sites, and oral histories of the people, of ceremonies, and of clans refer to these places at times when people still lived there. The Chacoan system is important to understanding who we Navajos are as a people, where we came from, and how we are related to the past, the present, and the future. They also tell us what our relationships are to other tribes, other peoples.

Figure 8.6. Fourth of July races in Chaco Canyon, 1934.

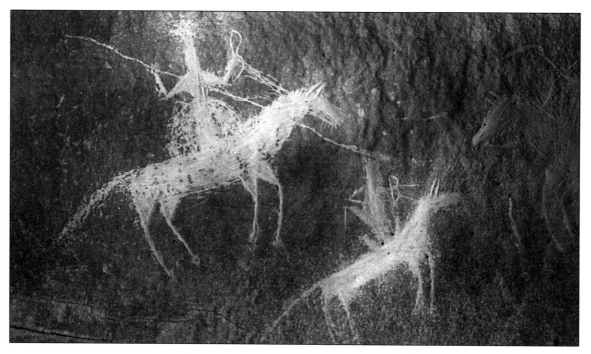

Figure 8.7. Navajo petroglyphs, Chaco Canyon.

There Is No End to Learning about Chaco Culture

The Navajo history of Chaco, the history of Chaco as told by other affiliated Native peoples, and indeed the history developed by archaeologists only touch the surface of the rich and complex tales that are embedded in these monumental structures and the surrounding landscapes. We are driven to try to uncover the stories, to understand the monuments, because we are human, but at some level we must recognize and accept that we may not be able to piece together the full history. Chaco culture encompassed a wide geographic expanse and involved many different groups of people. We are attempting to bring together different worldviews, different histories of the development and collapse of the Chaco system from many different perspectives.

We have some understanding of how the system was assembled, but little of why and how it functioned. The places we study, the places about which we have traditional histories—these places contain knowledge that has been hidden from us by the passage of time, the changes of seasons, and our manipulation of the landscape. In order to uncover that knowledge we must reexamine the existing record and reinterpret oral history in new and inventive ways. As scholars, traditional people, or "just people,"

we must continue to search for the untold narratives that have become part of the landscape. We must deepen our understanding of how oral narratives relate the cultural features to each other, to the natural landscape, and to forces of nature such as weather, groundwater, and celestial bodies. In doing so, we must protect all that is Chaco, not just the structures.

Acknowledgments

The clan and ceremonial information contained in this essay is part of the oral traditions that have been passed down in my family and community. The interpretation of the information is my own. Several colleagues—Robert M. Begay, Steven Begay, Taft Blackhorse, Klara B. Kelley, Anthony L. Klesert, Rena Martin, June-el Piper, and Miranda Warburton —reviewed drafts of this chapter. Their comments greatly improved and strengthened it.

Richard Begay has a bachelor's degree in anthropology from Dartmouth College and a master's of education from Harvard University's Graduate School of Education. He is from the communities of Crystal and Naschitti, New Mexico, and his clans are To'ahani, Tabaahi, Kin yaa'áanii, and Tachini. He currently lives in Phoenix, Arizona, where he works in the behavioral health field targeting urban Native Americans.

The *nine* Chaco Navajos

David M. Brugge

They came out of the north, along the Rocky Mountains, through the Great Basin, and across the western deserts, clad in buckskins and furs, with moccasins on their feet. The women drove dogs laden with their few goods, and the men defended them with their strong, sinew-backed bows. Even in winter they were moving, traveling on snowshoes. Sons and daughters of hunters, fishers, and gatherers in the far north, they mixed and mingled with the ancient farmers of the Southwest.

Arrival of the Apacheans

Their legends tell of fighting the Cliff Swallow people of Mesa Verde, eluding the Arrow People by the Sierra sin Agua, outwitting the haughty dwellers of Aztec and Salmon, freeing the slaves who built the massive houses in Chaco Canyon, and winning as wives the daughters of Tusayan. They call themselves Diné. In Spanish and English they are Navajos.

When they came is a matter of unending dispute. The language ties them to their Apache cousins and to the Athabaskan speakers of the boreal forest. They claim long residence on the southern Colorado Plateau, whereas those who dispute them say they arrived barely in advance of the Spanish conquistadors. Some theories lie between these extremes, making of seemingly simple stories more complex explanations. What is certain is that they and the Apaches virtually surrounded Pueblo country when they were first described by Spanish chroniclers. Their history since those early days is worthy of study, for it is one more testimonial to the tenacity of the human spirit.

Spanish Contact

The earliest descriptions of Navajo country more than encompass Chaco Canyon, as do all later accounts. For most of the 1600s, Spanish reports describe wars, wide cornfields, the taking of slaves, and one abortive attempt at conversion; however, the Navajos were lumped with the other Apacheans so regularly that their identity is blurred beyond sure recognition for decades at a time. We do know they were living west of the Rio Grande, clustered around Mount Taylor on the south, bordering the Hopis in the west, and south of the San Juan Mountains. Now mounted on horses, they traversed all the land between and doubtless some beyond.

Following the great Pueblo Revolt against Spanish rule in 1680 and the subsequent reconquest, the Navajos joined others in giving refuge to Pueblo people fleeing Spanish domination. Most of those who joined the Navajos settled in the Dinetah, a land east of present-day Farmington, New Mexico, on the upper San Juan River, where fertile fields produced crops of maize, squash, melons, beans, and cotton. It was there, too, that they first raised sheep. The refugees had brought herds of domestic animals, new crops, and religious lore. The population of the Dinetah grew, perhaps attracting Navajos from throughout their territory by its wealth and sophistication.

Wars with the Spaniards continued until a last Spanish incursion in 1716. Then the wealth of the Dinetah drew others. Utes and Comanches increasingly raided both Navajos and Spanish colonists. With a common enemy to fend off, peace broke out between these former enemies, to last some six decades.

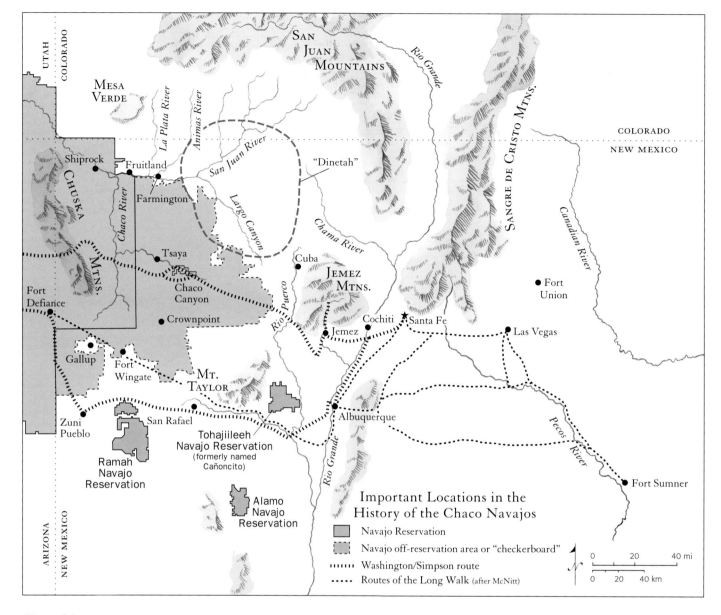

Figure 9.1.

The Dinetah and Chacra Mesa

With only Indian raiders to defend against, the Dinetah continued to prosper. With their Navajo hosts, the descendants of the refugees built small fortresses, today called *pueblitos* (little pueblos). They fired painted pots and wove fine baskets and warm woolen textiles. Their rock art depicts mounted warriors, dancing gods, constellations, birds, and beasts.

A population recently diminished by war and disease now multiplied and spread out over a vast region. On Chacra Mesa and in Chaco Canyon, pueblitos and hogans appeared, along with a reflection of the more elaborate rock art of the Dinetah.

War and Peace

The Spanish colonists prospered, too, and sought new land on which to plant their wheat and chilis and pasture their herds. They extended their settlements into the eastern fringes of Navajo country—not into the Dinetah but into Diné Bikéyah, the wider area of Navajo occupation. They promised to help ward off Ute raiders and were initially welcomed, but they did not integrate to form new clans as had the Pueblo refugees.

In the early 1750s, pressure from the Utes, combined with drought and growing internal discord, forced most Navajos to leave the Dinetah to join a

Figure 9.2. Pueblito site in the Dinetah.

Figure 9.3. Historic Navajo bread oven on Chacra Mesa.

steadily. The break came in 1773 when the Spanish governor formed an alliance with the Utes. The next year, Navajos drove the colonists out of their settlements all along the Rio Puerco of the East and around Mount Taylor.

In the 1750s, religious values that were part of a cultural revitalization influenced the Navajos who had left the Dinetah. A reassertion of old Apachean values is apparent in their lifeways at this time. Blessing Way became the dominant ceremony; it propounded a return to a simpler way of life. The anaasází, the ancestral "relatives" or "enemies," had built villages and made decorated pottery—and they were now gone. It seemed wise, then, that the Navajos, facing a threat to their own existence, give up Pueblo-style architecture and painted pottery. The people must be ready to move whenever drought, enemies, or ill fortune struck—such was the gods' decree.

Many accepted the teachings of the singers of Blessing Way, although a few still clung to the old ways. Archaeological evidence from late-eighteenth-century Navajo homesites on Chacra Mesa indicates a reluctance to make great changes. The Ute raids were probably less severe for these people, and the need to alter their lives might have been less strongly felt. The successes of the war of 1774–75 might have reinforced their faith in the old customs.

Then in 1781 came an event that some Navajos might well have regarded as Spanish vengeance: one of the worst smallpox epidemics on record swept through New Mexico, causing many deaths among the Pueblos. A sudden decrease in hogan construction on Chacra Mesa suggests that the devastation spread well beyond the boundaries of the Spanish colony.

Incursions into Navajo Country

Human inhabitation of the Chaco country in the late 1700s was sparse. The area became a buffer zone between the more densely occupied country to the south and west and the lands of old enemies.

growing population to the south and west. Navajo herds were also growing, a necessary adaptation when drought and warfare made farming a less secure means of feeding a family. Competition for land between Natives and whites grew slowly but

Into the 1800s, warfare between the Navajos and the Spanish colony escalated steadily. Chacra Mesa appears to have become a Navajo outpost, a staging area for trade, war, and diplomacy with the colony, and a base camp for hunting parties. A few families living at strategic locations made it possible for the tribe to maintain an early warning system so that herds could be moved to safety well before the arrival of enemy troops.

By the end of Spanish rule in Mexico in 1821, it seems probable that Chaco Canyon was a major military route into Navajo country. In 1823, when José Antonio Vizcarra led the first well-documented expedition down the canyon, he recorded a full set of Spanish place-names with no suggestion that he was applying them for the first time.

In 1849, after the Mexican War, Colonel John McCrae Washington's march from Santa Fe through northwestern New Mexico, so ably recorded by Lieutenant James H. Simpson and illustrated by the Kern brothers, benefited from knowledgeable guides, one of whom, called Sandoval, was a Navajo. Navajos who dealt with the expedition were experienced in watching troops follow west a route long used by invaders.

The initial efforts of US officials in dealing with the Navajos were no more effective than those of their Spanish and Mexican predecessors. They might have continued the same indecisive alternation between peace and war for decades had not the Civil War occasioned a buildup of federal forces in New Mexico. This military presence made campaigns against neighboring tribes more feasible than at any earlier time, and the Navajos, one of the largest free tribes in the West, became an early target.

In 1863, General James Carlton sent the Navajos an ultimatum requiring that they surrender and submit to removal from their country or face war. When no Navajos submitted to the order, Colonel Kit Carson, commanding nine companies of the First New Mexico Volunteers, was assigned the task of subduing the tribe, with Colonel J. Francisco Chávez commanding another four companies out of Fort Wingate. In addition, other tribes that could be persuaded to fight against the Navajos, such as the Utes, Western Apaches, Zunis, and Hopis, soon had warriors in the field. Hispanic raiders followed not far

behind. In the 1860s, more Navajo women and children were taken captive and baptized in village churches than ever before. In the winter of 1863–64, Navajos surrendered in large numbers and were taken on foot three hundred miles to Fort Sumner on the Pecos River in eastern New Mexico.

An oral tradition in the Chaco region relates that army wagons came to Pueblo Pintado to transport people into exile. Although Chaco Canyon lay outside the reservation created by the treaty of 1868—the year the Navajos were allowed to return to their homeland—families soon moved back to their original ranges.

Settlers, Traders, and Archaeologists

Hispanic and Anglo-American settlers began to move to the periphery of Chaco country in the 1870s, and stockmen from the new communities penetrated the hinterlands. Unsubstantiated reports place the LC and Carlisle cattle companies in the Chaco area by 1878. Sheepmen were nearby in 1882, and by 1884 sheep ranching by the Miera brothers of Cuba, New Mexico, had been extended to the vicinity. Navajos and whites began to vie for rights to rangeland.

Also in the 1880s, traders were moving beyond the already settled country to do business with the Navajos. In 1885 one trader established a post at Tiz-na-zin, ten miles west of Pueblo Bonito, and by 1889 Thomas Hye was trading at Pueblo Pintado. Traders in the countryside gave moral support to Navajo resistance to white encroachment—and sometimes the support was more than moral. By 1883 observers reported the Navajos to be well supplied with firearms, including up-to-date Winchesters and plenty of ammunition. Some had learned from professional soldiers how to use the new weapons during service as scouts in the Apache campaigns.

Even the federal government recognized Indians' right to peaceful use of public land. Indian agents were charged with enforcing this right but lacked the resources to do so and were faced with conflicting requirements that undermined their efforts. In 1892, agent E. H. Plummer issued several permits to Navajos to leave the reservation to gather salt and hunt. In the following year, he began to write permits for Navajos, including two men from Chaco Canyon, Welo and Navajo George, to remain on their land.

Figure 9.4. Navajo gathering at Wetherill trading post at Pueblo Bonito, September 1899.

In 1895, Richard Wetherill guided the Palmer family on an excursion to Chaco Canyon. Navajos lived all around the canyon and herded their sheep there. Wetherill returned in 1896 with George H. Pepper to commence archaeological excavations financed by the wealthy Hyde brothers of New York. The project, called the Hyde Exploring Expedition, gave local Navajo men what was probably their first experience with wage work. In addition, their wives found Pepper eager to purchase their woven blankets. He soon had them producing runners, decorative pillow covers, and even the first sandpainting tapestry. The visitors rented a stove from Welo.

Because Navajo workers encountered difficulty in cashing paychecks at nearby trading posts, the expedition began to pay its workmen in groceries during the second season's work, in 1897. This led Richard Wetherill and his wife, Marietta, to open a small trading post at Pueblo Bonito that fall, and the enterprise was enlarged the following summer as a joint venture by Wetherill and the Hyde brothers. There is a suggestion that the enterprising newcomers also began to raise sheep about this time, which would have placed them in competition with their Navajo customers for grazing rights. At about the turn of the century, the Hydes and Richard Wetherill began to expand their trading business and soon owned seventeen posts.

Land-use pressure from whites increased during this period, and each side accused the other of theft and trespass. By now, Anglos were gaining control of the sheep business, and two of them, T. D. Burns and his nephew, Edward Sargent, of the Chama region, held considerable political power in New Mexico. Their Hispanic herders followed a pattern of wintering their sheep in the Chaco country.

Opposition to the operations of the Hyde Exploring Expedition soon appeared. Edgar L. Hewett, a Santa Fe archaeologist, protested that the archaeological work done in 1900 amounted to vandalism. His objection may have been prompted in part by the fact that no professional archaeologist had been hired to replace Pepper, who did not return after 1899. Catholic priests at Saint Michael's Mission complained about Wetherill's dealings with the Navajos. Although some of the charges appear to have been exaggerated, there is clear evidence that Wetherill was arbitrary in his methods of debt collection and was alienating Navajo sympathies in this regard at least. His livestock holdings also appear to have been large enough to create conflict over range rights with both local Navajos and Hispanic herders.

Land Status

Land status in Chaco country was ill defined. The federal government had granted the Atlantic and Pacific Railroad all odd-numbered sections for fifty miles from the railroad right-of-way to the south, in order to help stimulate the development of a transcontinental railway system. This fifty-mile zone, known as the "checkerboard," extended to Chaco Canyon. The even-numbered sections and the land beyond to the north lay in the public domain.

The potential for conflict in this situation is readily apparent. Anglos and Hispanics felt they had the right to preempt any seemingly unoccupied land, whereas Indians believed their long if sporadic use of the land was sanctioned by their gods. In order to lessen conflict, methods of establishing legal rights had to be applied.

Although railroad land had legal status, Indian and white ranchers used most of it as freely as the public domain. White stockmen also began to lease or buy land from the railroad to improve their claim to the range. The first record of such efforts appears in 1901. Richard Wetherill and Frederick Hyde claimed homestead tracts in Chaco Canyon, and Marietta Wetherill reportedly purchased three sections from the railroad.

The earliest documented government action relating to land in the Chaco region was a temporary withdrawal in 1905 of two townships of thirty-six square miles each plus two additional one-square-mile sections in order to protect some of the ruins. The following year, an allotting agent began survey-ing 160-acre allotments to Navajos. Allotments were issued to individual Indians in trust status for twenty-five years. It was not until 1907 that a national monument was created to preserve the ruins. Toward the end of that year, President Theodore Roosevelt extended the reservation to the east. Agent William H. Harrison at Fort Defiance recommended that the federal government try to restrain the railroad's leasing and selling of land to white ranchers, because many Indians had unknowingly built their homes on railroad sections.

Bureau of Indian Affairs (BIA) officials recognized that the reservation extension would be short lived. They pushed the allotting program as rapidly as resources permitted, with the aim of placing most water sources under Navajo ownership and thereby giving the Indians control of most of the grazing land as well—a strategy white ranchers had long used elsewhere.

In addition, a new BIA superintendency was authorized. By April 1909, Samuel F. Stacher had assumed his duties as superintendent at Pueblo Bonito, where he intended to build a school, oversee the well-being of most of the eastern Navajos, and defend their rights to land. He initially rented office space and quarters from Richard Wetherill.

It did not take long for Stacher to realize that Wetherill's interests conflicted with those of the people under his charge. He found himself in increasingly serious controversy with Wetherill and his employees. Besides Wetherill's arbitrary methods of debt collection and competition with Navajos for rangeland, Stacher learned that Wetherill's employees were selling the Navajos liquor. Although it appears that the Wetherills were not personally involved in this last activity, it obviously did not help smooth relations. Stacher soon removed the superintendency from Chaco Canyon to Crownpoint.

The Killing of Richard Wetherill

Most Chaco Navajos had been involved in disputes of one sort or another with Wetherill. As early as Wetherill's second season in the canyon, old Welo found him ready to draw a gun merely to retain use of his rented stove—even though Welo had wished only to retrieve it temporarily for use during a ceremony. Navajo George, the oldest and wealthiest

Figure 9.5. Richard Wetherill's gravestone near Pueblo Bonito.

Navajo stockman in the area, had a long-standing dispute with Wetherill over a debt allegedly incurred by George's late wife.

Drastic events marked the year 1910. In February or March, Wetherill sold his trading post and leased his grazing land to a rancher from Gallup. While Wetherill was driving the rancher's cattle to Chaco Canyon, a Wetherill employee, Will Finn, rode west to take possession of a horse at Antonio Padilla's hogan. People tell widely varying stories today about who owned the horse, why Padilla had possession of it, and why Finn went to get it. In any case, the disagreement that arose over the ownership of the horse led to much more dramatic events.

Finn pistol-whipped Padilla and left him bleeding in front of his hogan. Padilla's wife sought the aid of her brother, Chiishch'ilin Biye'. Padilla appeared to be dead, and Chiishch'ilin Biye' set out to avenge his brother-in-law's presumed death, stopping at the Tsaya Trading post to buy ammunition for his rifle.

The Navajo urged his horse east along the road taken west by Wetherill, who had been joined by Finn, driving the cattle. When the opponents saw each other at a distance of about 150 yards, they exchanged several shots, and Wetherill fell from his horse. Chiishch'ilin Biye' then shot twice at Finn, who turned and fled to the Wetherill ranch house. Chiishch'ilin Biye' rode off to surrender to the superintendent at Shiprock. Behind him, a frightened group of whites barricaded themselves in the ranch house while their equally frightened Navajo neighbors sought safety on the mesa rims in camps they had used in the days of Kit Carson. Chiishch'ilin Biye' was tried and sentenced to prison for five to ten years but was released early because he suffered from tuberculosis.

Into the Modern Era

Wetherill's death did not greatly affect the course of events in the Chaco country. Others had acquired his interests, and new homesteaders arrived. In 1911, the eastern extension of the reservation was cancelled, and the allotting of land to Navajos ceased not long afterward. Stacher's efforts on behalf of the Navajos amounted to holding actions. He relied on allotments, compromises with the ranchers most likely to respect Navajo rights, and encouragement of the wealthier Navajos to lease railroad lands. His agreements with white ranchers helped some Navajos but aroused opposition from others who had to sacrifice land in order to effect land exchanges. Political pressures from white ranchers were so great, however, that Stacher had no alternative. One of them was Edward Sargent, who at the time was establishing his ranch east of the park.

A shrinking land base and a growing population placed great strains on the eastern Navajo economy. At Chaco Canyon, the *anaasází* ruins became one source of economic relief in 1921, when archaeological investigations were resumed. Local Navajos very much needed the jobs available at the excavations.

In 1929, the first full-time Park Service custodian, Hilding F. Palmer, arrived, and park projects became another source of employment. In the same year, a new allotting agent began work. He was able to survey about one hundred allotments per month for a little more than a year before political pressure from white ranchers forced the suspension of his program.

Meanwhile, Stacher promoted the more formal political organization of the Navajos in his jurisdiction through the creation of "chapters," a form of public meeting that the BIA hoped would foster cultural change. At the same time, many young whites, unable to obtain employment, were moving into the region to homestead, hoping that dry farming would succeed. Neither the Navajos nor the established white ranchers were happy to see them, but because most were veterans of World War I, overt resistance to this development would not have been politically expedient.

The deepening of the Great Depression brought about policy changes in the federal administration. As soon as he became president in 1933, Franklin D. Roosevelt instituted many large-scale government programs to provide employment, with National Park Service programs receiving high priority. Many of the early projects to halt erosion at Chaco Canyon employed young non-Indians from Pennsylvania and Sioux from the Dakotas. However, the BIA received separate funding for projects that hired local Navajos. For example, a Navajo ruins stabilization unit directed by Gordon Vivian worked not only in

Figure 9.6. A Navajo ruins stabilization unit, trained by Gordon Vivian, repairs the tower kiva at Kin Ya'a in about 1955.

the canyon but also on ruins throughout New Mexico and Arizona.

In spite of these beneficial projects, a different government program created greater animosity between Navajos and whites than had any event since the Fort Sumner exile. Conservationists had long recognized that overgrazing was harmful to western rangeland, and conservation was a prominent theme in many of the projects undertaken to stimulate the economy. Therefore the government instituted stock reduction programs throughout Navajo country. Although these efforts were based on a practical knowledge of range management, they revealed abysmal ignorance of the major role livestock played in Navajo culture. The programs severely damaged Navajo attitudes toward whites throughout Navajo country and created a genuinely disastrous situation for the off-reservation Navajos. As government employees removed or destroyed Navajo stock, white ranchers who were not subject to the same regulations brought in new animals to graze the range.

Measures to consolidate land holdings to create separate Navajo and white areas had been only marginally successful, despite Stacher's most strenuous efforts. The Roosevelt administration proposed a boundary bill to settle the matter by extending the reservation and leasing the rest of the country to the white ranchers. BIA officials even promised reservation status to the checkerboard Navajos in exchange for voluntary stock reduction. When repeated efforts to get the extension bill through Congress failed, the eastern Navajos became the strongest opponents of the federal proposals, defeating a planned reorganization of the tribal government in a hard-fought election and then helping elect as tribal chairman Jacob C. Morgan, a staunch foe of the government programs.

The effects of stock reduction and loss of land brought poverty of a sort that few Navajos had experienced for many years. The Park Service fenced Chaco Canyon National Monument and evicted the Navajo families living within its boundaries. The Navajos keenly felt the loss of range, and had the park not been a source of jobs, the result would probably have been catastrophic.

Figure 9.7. A Navajo family in a horse-drawn wagon, about 1950. In the distance, a work crew erects a power line.

After the Japanese attack on Pearl Harbor brought the United States into World War II, Navajo attitudes toward the war varied. In time, however, many Navajos served in the armed forces, some as code talkers in the Pacific theater, using the Navajo language as an unbreakable code. Many more worked in defense industries. As a result, the tribe enjoyed renewed prosperity. Because of the demands for manpower, no custodian remained at the monument, and some Navajos evicted earlier moved back to their old homes temporarily. Again Blessing Way ceremonies were held, this time to pray for the safety of young Navajos overseas.

The effects of World War II on the Navajos extended beyond the defeat of the Japanese and Germans. Returning servicemen, servicewomen, and war workers placed a sudden burden on the resources of the land, and the veterans were made dramatically aware of the production limits of their homeland. As they competed for jobs, they also sharply felt the poor preparation they had received in school. The crisis that followed the war affected the Navajo economy much as the Depression had. A new understanding of

the world beyond the four sacred mountains led to a readier acceptance of education and, within a few years, a remarkable growth in schools and school attendance.

Oil discoveries, uranium mining, and the exploitation of other minerals brought a rapid increase in tribal wealth. The tribal government dedicated a significant proportion of this money to scholarships. The eastern Navajos experienced still another gain. As the white ranchers aged, they sought to retire by selling the ranches that their children did not want. Perhaps the most important acquisition for the people living around Chaco Canyon was the tribe's 1958 purchase of the Sargent ranches. Although the Navajos undoubtedly felt pride in this tribal action, the return of the surface rights on these ranches was insufficient to solve local people's land problems. Today the land is held in fee simple, and the tribe, as a corporate entity, pays taxes on it, as would any private owner of real estate. The tribe leases the grazing rights for separate tracts to several individual Navajos, only a few of whom are from local families.

Today, the expansion of mining activities also threatens the homes and rangeland of many Chaco Navajos. The federal government and the railroad hold mineral rights to large coal, oil, and uranium deposits other than those beneath their allotments. Proposals to develop these deposits are disputed and in some cases have been abandoned, at least for the present. A people still working to catch up with the education of the general population now faces possible loss of land needed to preserve a way of life.

The uncertainties of the Chaco Navajos' tenuous hold on the land, which have persisted for so long, seem destined to linger for some time. Questions remain about whether an ultimate resolution of the matter will be found, and if so, whether it will result in the acquisition of secure Navajo title. There can be little doubt, however, that with each performance of Blessing Way in the eastern Navajo region, prayers are repeated for the return of land within the domain of the sacred mountains.

David M. Brugge, an anthropologist and recognized authority on Athabaskans in the Southwest, is retired from the National Park Service. He has written *A History of the Navajos.*

Figure 10.1. The great house at Casamero village, near Prewitt, New Mexico.

Great-House Communities and the Chaco World

John Kantner

More than forty-three miles to the south of Chaco Canyon, nestled against the red sandstone walls of the Red Mesa Valley, is a small village that archaeologists call Casamero. When its first permanent inhabitants arrived, sometime in the 700s CE, they built pithouses on top of the mesa; later, they constructed a loose cluster of small masonry houses at the base of the cliffs. These modest structures, none encompassing more than a dozen rooms, had roughly shaped walls made of the readily available sandstone. By the 900s, Casamero consisted of no more than twenty of these houses. Its inhabitants, however, had many neighbors in similar villages scattered in all directions along the south-facing cliffs. These villages included Andrews, two and a half miles to the southeast, and Blue J, less than a mile and a half to the northeast. In many of these villages, large pit structures, or "great kivas," served as centers of communal ceremonial, social, and political activity.

At some point in the late 900s or early 1000s, the residents of Casamero built something new—a two-story structure of more than twenty rooms. Constructed of carefully shaped limestone blocks fitted together into massive walls, the new building had unusually large rooms enclosing a plaza. At about the same time, their neighbors at Andrews put up a comparable building, and preliminary research at Blue J suggests that its residents augmented an older house by adding thick limestone walls similar to those at Casamero. This new architectural form appeared in virtually every village throughout the Red Mesa Valley, just as it did in more than two hundred other communities across the northern

Southwest in the tenth and eleventh centuries. To archaeologists today, the masonry work, exceptional size, and time period of these buildings suggest that they were inspired by the great-house architecture of Chaco Canyon. We therefore refer to the region in which these buildings appear as the "Chaco world," reflecting our assumption that great houses both within and outside the canyon were part of the same cultural phenomenon.

History of Chaco World Research

Acknowledgment of the importance of Chacoan architecture outside Chaco Canyon did not come easily to archaeologists. In 1881, one of the founders of American anthropology, Lewis Henry Morgan, noted the similarity between the ruins of Chaco Canyon and those found at Aztec, sixty-two miles to the north. The archaeologist Earl H. Morris, who excavated at Aztec Ruins between 1917 and 1921, demonstrated that Chacoan material culture was not confined to the canyon. Frank H. H. Roberts reached the same conclusion while working at Chimney Rock Pueblo in southwestern Colorado and Village of the Great Kivas in west-central New Mexico. Their views, however, did not substantially influence interpretations of Chaco Canyon, where other archaeologists were conducting research throughout the first decades of the 1900s. Most experts thought that "outlying" Chacoan features reflected only the movement of small groups of people away from the canyon. No one really considered the possibility that the entire region was integrated into a single political system.

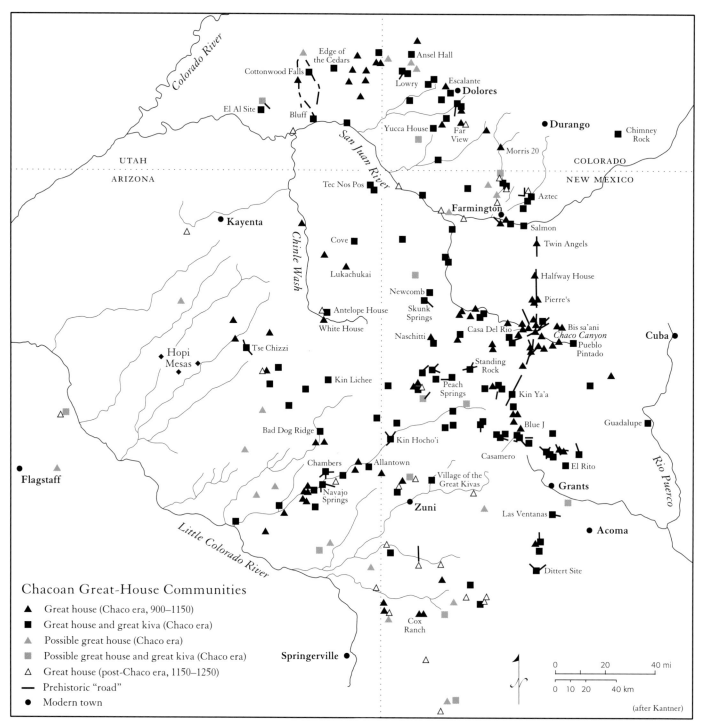

Figure 10.2.

Chacoan Great-House Communities

▲ Great house (Chaco era, 900–1150)
■ Great house and great kiva (Chaco era)
▲ Possible great house (Chaco era)
■ Possible great house and great kiva (Chaco era)
△ Great house (post-Chaco era, 1150–1250)
— Prehistoric "road"
● Modern town

Map labels: Colorado River, Edge of the Cedars, Ansel Hall, Cottonwood Falls, Lowry, Escalante, Dolores, El Al Site, Bluff, San Juan River, Yucca House, Far View, Durango, Chimney Rock, UTAH, ARIZONA, COLORADO, NEW MEXICO, Morris 20, Tec Nos Pos, Aztec, Kayenta, Farmington, Salmon, Chinle Wash, Cove, Twin Angels, Lukachukai, Halfway House, Newcomb, Pierre's, Skunk Springs, Antelope House, White House, Casa Del Rio, Bis sa'ani, Chaco Canyon, Cuba, Naschitti, Pueblo Pintado, Hopi Mesas, Tse Chizzi, Standing Rock, Kin Lichee, Peach Springs, Kin Ya'a, Bad Dog Ridge, Blue J, Guadalupe, Kin Hocho'i, Casamero, El Rito, Flagstaff, Chambers, Allantown, Village of the Great Kivas, Grants, Navajo Springs, Zuni, Las Ventanas, Acoma, Rio Puerco, Dittert Site, Little Colorado River, Cox Ranch, Springerville

0 20 40 mi
0 10 20 40 km
N
(after Kantner)

Through the middle of the twentieth century, archaeologists continued to find Chacoan architecture outside Chaco Canyon, but not until the 1970s did they recognize the potential significance of these discoveries. Two archaeological projects were instrumental in changing the prevailing view of Chacoan outliers. The Chaco Center (a collaboration of the National Park Service and the University of New Mexico) and the Public Service Company of New Mexico each sponsored extensive great-house inventories of the San Juan Basin. The findings of their researchers, who trekked many miles of desert terrain, were published in two independent volumes that between them described approximately fifty great houses. Other institutions conducted excavations at a handful of these sites, including Guadalupe Ruin, sixty-two miles southeast of Chaco Canyon; Salmon Ruin, forty-three miles to the north; and Bis sa'ani, twelve miles to the east. Additional research in the 1970s focused on a network of "roads" then thought to connect great houses across the San Juan Basin.

In a 1978 article, Jeffrey Altschul proposed a new idea—that the central canyon formed the center of an "interaction sphere." Archaeologists no longer regarded Chaco Canyon as an isolated phenomenon but rather as part of an extensive system in which goods and information flowed between outlying communities and the central canyon. This viewpoint informed research across the Chaco world through the 1980s and into the 1990s.

A recent step in Chaco world research occurred during the Chaco Synthesis Project, which began in the late 1990s. It consisted of a series of seminars that were intended to wrap up more than two decades of Chaco Center research. I helped organize one seminar, appropriately titled "The Chaco World," during which we attempted to consolidate as much data as possible on all great-house research conducted outside of Chaco Canyon. The resulting spatial database, representing more than two hundred Chacoan great houses, is available on the World Wide Web (http://sipapu.gsu.edu/chacoworld.html) and is continually revised as new information becomes available.

What Do All the Terms Mean?

"Outliers," "great houses," "great-house communities"—we use a variety of terms to describe the manifestation of Chacoan patterns outside Chaco Canyon itself. Most reflect the way views of the Chaco world have changed over the past several decades, resulting in considerable confusion even among professionals. Like most of my colleagues, I characterize a "great house," whether inside or outside Chaco Canyon, as an unusually massive, multistory building with large rooms and thick masonry walls. Other features that distinguish a great house from a typical Puebloan residence of the late ninth through the early twelfth century include circular kivas built inside the structure (rather than out in the plaza), roadways, earthen

platforms and berms, and nearby great kivas. I consider Pueblo Bonito and its neighbor, Chetro Ketl, to be the archetypal great houses, in contrast to those found outside the canyon, which are much smaller.

We use the term "outlier"—the word became popular during the inventories of the 1970s and early 1980s—to describe great houses located outside of Chaco Canyon. Occasionally, "outlier" refers to both a great house and the cluster of homes—the village—in which it was built. In recent years, however, some of my colleagues and I have protested the use of this term, for it implies a subservient and passive relationship between Chaco Canyon great houses and those found elsewhere; such a relationship has yet to be scientifically demonstrated. As a result, some of us prefer other terminology, such as "Chacoan great house" and "great-house community," to refer, respectively, to the great houses found outside Chaco Canyon and to their accompanying villages. These terms convey the cultural connections between the central canyon and the rest of the Chaco world without implying exactly how they were connected.

Great-House Communities across Space and Time

The debate over what to call great houses and their communities is largely due to the fact that so little is known about them. Archaeologists presently know of more than 225 possible great houses located outside Chaco Canyon, but surprisingly few of these exhibit all of the expected features listed previously. Their only consistent characteristic is that they are comparatively more massive than the residential structures around them. Some appear to have large rooms; others do not. Some have multiple stories; others do not. The association of roadways, great kivas, berms, and other features also varies. Even within a single great house, considerable inconsistency exists: at the Blue J great house where I am working, some walls are thin while others are massive. To further complicate the matter, archaeologists have excavated only a handful of these sites. To positively identify and date a great house without digging is more an art than a science.

Despite these problems, some interesting patterns do appear when one plots all the suspected great houses on a map of the northern Southwest (you can explore this yourself using the online great-

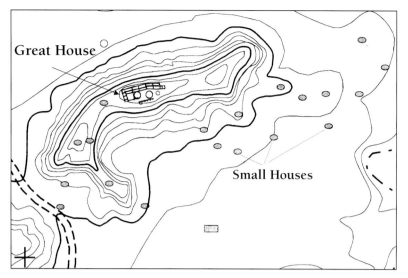

Figure 10.3. Distribution of dwellings in the Guadalupe great-house community.

house database referred to earlier). For example, all but a small handful are associated with sizable clusters of homes, and the vast majority of great houses were built in already established Puebloan villages. The case of Bis sa'ani, a so-called scion outlier, is rare in the Chaco world: this great house and its accompanying community were built all at once. Typically, a group of ancestral Pueblos established its great house in the center of a village, usually in a prominent topographical location. While such locations might have provided the best views of the surrounding landscape, they also had the disadvantage of being exposed to the greatest extremes of weather. Residents of the Blue J community, for example, built their great house on the westernmost edge of the community, where the best views are found, but the location is fully exposed to fierce winds.

The most impressive great houses are located within the San Juan Basin. Kin Ya'a, for example, is particularly striking. Located a bit more than twenty-five miles southwest of Chaco Canyon, this great house once included more than forty rooms built of massive masonry. One of the four original kivas built into the structure is a "tower kiva" that still stands nearly four stories tall. A dense community of eighty homes clusters closely around Kin Ya'a. In contrast, the Cove great house lies seventy-eight miles northwest of Chaco Canyon, well beyond the boundaries of the San Juan Basin. Its builders created a small, single-story structure of eighteen rooms

and a more modest style of masonry. An unassuming community of about thirty households surrounds it.

In her research, Ruth Van Dyke uncovered another compelling spatial pattern in the Chaco world: great houses in the San Juan Basin generally are not associated with great kivas, but they do consistently include plazas enclosed on at least three sides by walls. This mirrors the pattern found in Chaco Canyon and suggests that ties between the canyon and its nearest neighbors in the San Juan Basin were comparatively strong. It also indicates that people in the basin preferred visiting the monumental canyon great houses instead of using local great kivas, which were the traditional ceremonial centers of ancestral Puebloan communities. Beyond the boundaries of the San Juan Basin, in contrast, great kivas become more frequent, even in great-house communities. Van Dyke's discoveries about great-house distribution patterns increase our understanding of the emergence of Chaco Canyon and its world.

Great houses exhibit interesting patterns across time as well as space. In general, Chacoan architecture appeared first in the San Juan Basin, and only much later were great houses built in communities well beyond it. We find the earliest outlying great houses, such as Casa del Rio and Padilla Well, in the very heart of the San Juan Basin, not far from Chaco Canyon itself. Around the middle 900s, people began to construct great houses on the southern edges of the San Juan Basin and in the Red Mesa Valley. As the archaeologist Gwinn Vivian suggests, the inhabitants of this region had historical and social ties to Chaco Canyon, and as they visited one another, the idea of the great house passed to the south from neighbor to neighbor. Great-house construction spread relatively quickly down the drainage of the Rio Puerco of the West in the late 900s, into the foothills of the Chuska Mountains by about 1000, and north into the San Juan River area beginning in the mid-1000s. Bursts of great-house construction occurred throughout the Chaco region in the latter half of the eleventh century. This was a time when activity in Chaco Canyon itself was reaching a frenzied level. By the

Figure 10.4. This staircase at the west end of Chaco Canyon, cut into bedrock, leads to Ahshilepah Canyon and then probably to Hogback outlier.

turn of the twelfth century, thousands of people—both within and outside the central canyon—were building and using great houses.

The Famous Chacoan Roads

No aspect of the Chaco world has generated more public interest and yet such confusion as the "roads" or "roadways" that are associated with many great houses. Archaeologists recognized the roads in the late 1800s and early 1900s, erroneously interpreting the wide, shallow swales they saw as ancient irrigation canals. Although the roadways can measure up to thirty-three feet in width, they can be nearly invisible at ground level, because their builders for the most part simply scraped away soil and mounded it along the sides. The roads can be seen better from the air, particularly when the sun is low in the sky and shadows are most visible. In the 1970s and early 1980s, researchers used techniques such as aerial photography and infrared scanning to map what they thought were well over a hundred miles of prehistoric roads. Using these methods, they perceived extensive networks of roads, which they interpreted as physically linking most great houses to Chaco Canyon. This image of the Chacoan landscape persists today in much of the popular literature.

Later, in the 1980s, when archaeologists attempted to verify the existence of all these roads, they discovered problems in the original interpretations. Close examination on the ground revealed that many of the alignments were actually historic roads. Others that seemed to be visible in aerial photographs simply could not be found. The lack of artifacts associated with some of the previously mapped roads made their existence even more suspect. By the 1990s, criticisms of the original assessments had begun to appear in print. Bureau of Land Management archaeologist John Roney, for example, noted that the vast majority of confirmed roads extended no more than a few kilometers.

Indeed, at the present time, researchers can confirm only one continuous roadway of any length: the famous "North Road" that extends north from Chaco Canyon across forty-three miles of the San Juan Basin, to end abruptly at the edge of Kutz Canyon (see map, p. xii). The "South Road," which runs thirty-seven miles southwest from Chaco Canyon to the prominent Hosta Butte, also is reasonably complete. All other confirmed Chaco-era roads are simply short snippets. In my computer-based research, I found that the road builders were not concerned with selecting cost-efficient routes between villages.

Instead, they designed some roadways to connect ceremonial architecture, whereas many others simply provided central "avenues" through communities. Still others symbolically articulated with prominent topographical features, much the way the South Road from Chaco ends at Hosta Butte.

Despite the evolving interpretations of Chacoan roads, they are still impressive features. One of their most cited characteristics is their linearity. Many segments, such as the North Road, proceed in reasonably straight lines, often disregarding local topography in order to preserve their trajectory. In a few cases, roads employ ramps or staircases to go over obstacles rather than going around them. Although the road builders primarily cleared soil to create the roads, they also created raised beds, stairways, and ramps, especially around Chaco Canyon. Many stairways and even some roadbeds were cut directly into sandstone cliffs. The ancestral Puebloans also constructed architectural features along the sides of the roadways, including earthworks and *herraduras*, horseshoe-shaped masonry enclosures that can measure more than twenty feet across. Although the once-hypothesized "network" of Chacoan roads has yet to be confirmed, the amount of labor that ancestral Puebloans committed to constructing the alignments and their associated features was extraordinary.

Life in Great-House Communities

As we learn more about the Chaco world, we are beginning to investigate how great-house communities interacted with one another and with the apparent center in Chaco Canyon. Two decades ago, H. Wolcott Toll and other researchers convincingly demonstrated that the inhabitants of the central canyon acquired great quantities of finished goods and raw materials from virtually all parts of the Chaco world (see chapter 5). Ceramics, timber, exotic goods, and perhaps even food flowed regularly into Chaco Canyon, presumably supplied by the residents of outlying great-house communities. Few goods, if any, however, moved back out of the canyon, a conclusion I have corroborated in my investigations at the Blue J great-house community. Thus, it seems, the people of Chaco Canyon were consumers, not middlemen or distributors of resources. Following these discoveries, many of us now view Chaco Canyon as a pilgrimage center that routinely received visitors bearing gifts.

Some archaeologists are learning that interaction among great-house communities in the San Juan Basin was quite variable. For example, researchers working in the southern basin and the Red Mesa Valley are finding that most villagers interacted primarily with their immediate neighbors and rarely received goods from more distant parts of the Chaco world. Exotic materials such as turquoise and shell beads, of course, did flow in modest quantities across the entire region, but ancestral Puebloan people had always exchanged such items. Social, political, and economic life in great-house communities was apparently a local affair, even at the height of activity in Chaco Canyon itself.

What happened in the great houses outside Chaco Canyon? This question remains largely unanswered, just as it does for the long-studied great houses in the central canyon. Kathy Roler Durand, an archaeologist from Eastern New Mexico University, recently noted that comparatively large quantities of unusual artifacts—effigy vessels, carved wooden staffs or "wands," stone phalluses, and many bird remains, including those of a few macaws—have been found at the handful of outlier great houses excavated by archaeologists. This led her to conclude that great houses were at least storehouses for ceremonial items, if not the actual locations of important rituals. Associated features such as the linear roadways, enclosed plazas, and encircling berms also evoke images of ceremonial activity. My overall impression is that outlying great houses served as the ceremonial hearts of villages in the Chacoan region and were local expressions of the much more imposing architecture of Chaco Canyon.

The Direction of Chaco World Research

Archaeologists working in Chacoan studies disagree about many things, but all concur that much more research remains to be done on the outlying great houses and great-house communities before we will be able to understand what the Chaco phenomenon was about. And only by scientifically excavating more sites will we be able to answer some of the more pressing questions. We can address other unresolved issues, however, by taking further advantage of new

Figure 10.5. Among the more than two hundred great houses that have been identified are some well-known monuments such as White House (pictured above) in Canyon de Chelly and Far View in Mesa Verde National Park.

technologies. Studies employing geographic information systems—computer databases in which detailed information can be tied to digital, three-dimensional landscapes—are already answering questions about the roadways and the function of the tower kivas that the Chacoans built into a few of their great houses. Increasingly sophisticated techniques in remote sensing are pinpointing Chacoan features from space and penetrating thick soil deposits to reveal what lies below the surface at great houses. Geochemical techniques applied to pottery, stone, and even wood and corn are now telling us where items of trade originated and where they ended up as people interacted across the Chaco world. Just as the past few decades of outlier research revolutionized our understanding of the Chaco system, the next few decades promise to be exciting as we continue doing research in the northern Southwest.

John Kantner, an associate professor of anthropology at Georgia State University, is director of the Lobo Mesa Archaeological Project, which focuses on the Chacoan Pueblo people who inhabited northwestern New Mexico between 850 and 1150. With Nancy M. Mahoney, he co-edited *Great House Communities across the Chacoan Landscape*, which appeared in 2000.

Figure 11.1. A horseshoe-shaped shrine above the Candelaria site, looking toward Mount Taylor.

eleven

Chaco's Sacred Geography

Ruth M. Van Dyke

Chaco Canyon engulfs the contemporary visitor in emptiness. From atop Pueblo Alto, the horizon stretches away in sedimentary waves lapping against the distant shores of the Chuska Mountains and the Dutton Plateau. On a sun-scoured summer morning, the stillness is broken only by the overhead whoosh of a raven's wings. It is ironic that visitors should value Chaco for its silence today, because prehistorically the canyon must have been filled with sound—chattering voices, barking dogs, and the repetitive rasp of corn ground against rock. Envision the canyon humming with preparations as people poured in from all directions to celebrate—what? Many archaeologists today believe Chaco Canyon was a place for ceremonies on a large scale and that people traveled to Chaco from outlying areas in order to witness or participate in rituals there. But what was the nature of their beliefs? Although we can never know any specifics about ceremonies, the Chacoans did leave us tantalizing hints about the major ideas behind their worldview, inscribed in architecture and landscape.

Many people today, including and perhaps especially many Native Americans, feel a particular connection to the Southwestern landscape. In his book *Wisdom Sits in Places* (University of New Mexico Press, 1996), the anthropologist Keith Basso eloquently describes how elements of the landscape figure into stories that lend meaning and morality to the lives of Western Apaches. The Chacoans, too, must have felt the dramatic effects of the mesas and badlands, canyons and volcanic spires of the central San Juan Basin. Like all peoples, they undoubtedly ascribed stories and meanings to the world around

them. We cannot know the plots and protagonists of those stories, but we can learn a little about what ideas were important to the Chacoans simply by looking at the ways in which they emphasized and altered the spatial world around them.

Keys to understanding the Chacoans' sacred geography are found in the beliefs of many contemporary and ethnographically known Pueblo peoples. The Tewas, Keres, Zunis, and Hopis place importance on spatial divisions and directions, dividing their physical, social, and spiritual worlds into horizontal and vertical dimensions of cosmologies expressed through landscape and architecture. Multiple levels of social and spiritual meaning are inscribed on the landscape by topographic features and shrines, and the pueblo itself represents this organization in microcosm. Horizontal divisions correspond to cardinal directions, and vertical divisions include upper and lower worlds. Nested layers or symmetrical quarters are connected at a center place—the pueblo. The center place is the place of convergence, where six sacred directions (four cardinal directions plus zenith and nadir) join and where symmetrically opposing forces are balanced.

The Chacoan Landscape

The contemporary Pueblo world cannot be considered a direct reflection of the Chacoan past. Nevertheless, some vital elements of Pueblo ideology, including notions of balance and center place, are clearly represented on the Chacoan landscape. The Chacoans constructed buildings, roads, and shrines that expressed their ideas about the organization of the world. They also used elements of the natural topography to dramatic effect. The result was a landscape that was built to be experienced, to express ideas about sacred directions and dualistic balance. Oppositional dualisms such as those between the celestial and the subterranean, the visible and the invisible, and north and south are represented in Chacoan great houses, great kivas, road alignments, earthworks, and shrines. The canyon itself was the center place, the fulcrum that balanced opposing forces, the intersection of sacred directions, the axis mundi around which both space and time revolved.

On the gray-green expanses of the Colorado Plateau, ancient sediments have settled into horizontal beds riven by erosion into canyons, mesas, and occasionally fantastic spires. The sun sears this world to monochrome at midday, and in the evening, low-angle light pours liquid gold over distant cliffs. On this open, light-filled landscape, it is not surprising that visibility was important to the Chacoans in a number of respects. There are line-of-sight connections among buildings, shrines, and topographic features. Highly visible "up" places represent the zenith direction. And the visible is dualistically opposed to the invisible: Chacoans manipulated the positions of sites and features to juxtapose the observable and the hidden.

Although the word "canyon" denotes a low place, Chaco Canyon is both a low place and an exceptionally high place, located in the geographic center of the San Juan Basin. The Chaco River created the canyon as it cut through the north side of Chacra Mesa, a long, uplifted cuesta four hundred to five hundred feet high that runs for forty miles east-west across the central basin. Chacra Mesa breaks at Fajada Gap and at South Gap to form South Mesa and West Mesa, respectively. On clear days, some of the most spectacular vistas in northwestern New Mexico can be seen from the high places atop the canyon. To the north jut the snowcapped peaks of the San Juans and the distinctive rippled hump of Huérfano Mountain. To the west, badlands and volcanic plugs guard the long blue line of the Chuska Mountains. To the south, Hosta Butte and Little Hosta Butte rise to oversee the line of the Dutton Plateau. To the southeast rises the piebald cone of Mount Taylor. The juxtaposition of the hidden,

invisible, protected canyon with these dramatic high points created a topographic tension between high and low, between the hidden and the visible—a relationship the Chacoans referenced and exploited.

In a study of Aboriginal Australian landscapes included in Wendy Ashmore and Bernard Knapp's *Archaeologies of Landscape* (Blackwell, 1999), Paul Taçon notes that people tend to attach special significance to sites of dramatic topographic change—where earth and sky are strikingly juxtaposed—or places that afford varied or panoramic vistas. Such a place may be considered an axis mundi, a place at which different worlds or levels of existence intersect. In the San Juan Basin, the Chacoans celebrated and amplified the visual drama, the juxtaposition of earth and sky, through placement of great houses, shrines, and stone circles. These features often were situated to emphasize line-of-sight connections between the canyon, outlying great houses, and key topographic landmarks such as Hosta Butte. In their 1970s survey of Chaco Canyon, Alden Hayes and Tom Windes discovered an extensive system of shrines providing intervisibility among canyon great houses. A shrine atop Huérfano Mountain visually links Chaco Canyon with its most distant northeastern outlier, the astronomically significant site of Chimney Rock. A horseshoe-shaped shrine at the edge of El Malpais, a volcanic lava flow near the outlier called Candelaria, faces Mount Taylor and links this area with shrines and outliers in the Red Mesa Valley. And a group of cairns at the end of West Mesa connects Chaco Canyon with nearly the entire western half of the San Juan Basin.

Visibility and Great Houses
Visibility is one of the key characteristics of Chacoan great houses, both within and outside the canyon. As the archaeologists John Stein, Stephen Lekson, Michael Marshall, and others have noted, the Chacoans built their great houses to see from and to be seen. These buildings dominate the visual landscape through their immense size, elevated position, or opportunistic use of dramatic topography. Massive canyon great houses such as Pueblo Bonito dwarf the viewer. Tsin Kletsin, built atop South Mesa in the early 1100s, is situated to maximize intervisibility with other great houses and shrines. From Peñasco

Figure 11.2. Tsin Kletsin, a great house built on South Mesa in the early 1100s.

Blanco, located high on a West Mesa terrace four miles west of Pueblo Bonito, nearly all of "downtown" Chaco can be seen. Some outlier great houses, such as Pueblo Pintado, Kin Bineola, Salmon, and Aztec West, overwhelm the viewer with massive, three- to four-story walls and layouts that encompass hundreds of rooms.

The three-story Kin Bineola great house is an excellent example of visual prominence achieved through sheer mass. One of the biggest great houses outside Chaco Canyon, Kin Bineola has a footprint of approximately 36,000 square feet and a total estimated floor area of nearly 88,500 square feet. It contains 105 ground-floor rooms, 58 second-floor rooms, 34 third-floor rooms, three hallways, eight ground-story enclosed kivas, two upper-story enclosed kivas, and two enclosed plazas. Kin Bineola's builders created still more mass by using "double" wall construction on the western exterior of the great house. There, they separated two core-and-veneer walls with twenty to thirty inches of empty space divided into cells. These rooms have no ostensible purpose other than to make an already imposing edifice appear to be even bigger.

Other outlier great houses are small, unimposing, single-story buildings of twenty rooms, but they are situated in dramatic, imposing locales on high ridges or mesas, overlooking a community below. Examples include the sites of Guadalupe and Escalon. A few outliers contain the ultimate in outlier visibility—a tower kiva. A true tower kiva is a cylinder of four kivas stacked one upon the other. As Jesse Walter Fewkes suggested as early as 1917, tower kivas seem likely to represent ancestral Pueblo stories of emergence through multiple worlds. At the outlier Kin Klizhin, the distinctive form of the tower kiva is visible for miles in every direction, as well as from various vantage points atop South and West Mesas.

Visibility and lines of sight continually shift as people move across the landscape. Some access routes into Chaco Canyon juxtapose the hidden and the visible. For example, on an approach from the North Road, Pueblo Alto is visible for many miles, but Pueblo Bonito, Chetro Ketl, and the other structures on the canyon floor are not visible until one passes Pueblo Alto and nears the north rim of Chaco Canyon. On an approach along the South Road, Pueblo de Arroyo is neatly framed through South

Figure 11.3. Escalon, an outlier great house that sits high in an imposing location.

of the canyon as the center place at the intersection of both vertical and horizontal planes. We have already seen that Chaco Canyon sits at the geographic heart of the San Juan Basin. This centrality—already present when the great-house builders began their work—may be one reason why Chaco became such an important location. The Chacoans subsequently constructed other elements of directional expression emphasizing the canyon as center place. Four horizontal directions are expressed most obviously through roads and to some extent through building alignments and orientations.

Gap, but few other canyon great houses are visible until one is nearly through the gap. This interplay between the visible and the invisible emphasizes Chaco as the center place, the place of balance between opposing, dualistic extremes.

Another way in which the visible is juxtaposed with the invisible is through the association of great houses and great kivas. Great houses are rectangular, aboveground spaces to which, in some cases, access may have been restricted. During the Classic Bonito phase (1020–1100), great kivas were built in association with great houses at Pueblo Bonito, Una Vida, Peñasco Blanco, Chetro Ketl, and Hungo Pavi. In the circular, semisubterranean space of a great kiva, a few hundred people could have gathered to participate in or witness events taking place there. Great kivas also were constructed in association with great houses in countless outlier communities. The juxtaposition of great houses and great kivas symbolically balanced aboveground, visible, restricted space against subterranean, invisible, open space, representing zenith and nadir in a scheme of sacred directions and creating a set of dualistic tensions on the landscape, with the canyon or plaza as center place.

Horizontal directions, too, are inscribed on the Chacoan landscape, suggesting that Chacoans thought

The Chacoan "Roads"

"Roads," or cleared linear alignments, have long been recognized across the Chacoan world, but the functions of these enigmatic features have been much debated. In the 1980s, researchers hypothesized that roads extended out from Chaco like the spokes of a wheel. However, subsequent ground-verification efforts by the Bureau of Land Management demonstrated that the road network was not as complete or extensive as once thought. The alignments do not primarily connect Chaco with outliers or with resources; rather, many extend but a short distance from a great house before disappearing. John Roney and others have argued convincingly that the alignments were not meant primarily as routes of transportation but rather were part of an iconic or symbolic package of "Bonito-style" architectural features that included great houses, great kivas, and earthworks. Of course, this does not mean that people did not walk on the alignments. Compacted surfaces of any sort, including trails, are easier to walk on than the soft dune sands that surround Chaco to the north and south. And again, road alignments entering Chaco Canyon condition the pedestrian approach to maximize the juxtaposition of the visible and the invisible.

Figure 11.4. Aerial view of three prehistoric roads converging on Pueblo Alto. A fourth road passes to the left of the site.

and South Gap are possibilities), road segments visibly traverse the terrain from the canyon past the outliers of Bee Burrow and Kin Ya'a. The South Road stops three miles short of Hosta Butte, a dramatically visible landform framed from Chaco through South Gap. The South Road could logically represent the visible, the living, and the vertical.

The directions east and west were less elaborated; this dimension might have been represented by the east-west-trending canyon itself. An East Road may have run down the length of the canyon from Fajada Butte to the massive great house of Pueblo Pintado. Although vehicle traffic and erosion may well have obscured most traces of such a road, segments are visible near Pueblo Pintado and Chaco East. Chaco Wash provides a conduit to the west, toward the Chuska Mountains, source of many commodities found in Chaco Canyon, including timber, trachyte-tempered ceramics, and Narbona Pass chert. Clearly, the cairn complex at the west end of West Mesa emphasizes that this direction was an important approach to the canyon. Although a West Road is not well defined and continuous, a number of suggestive segments exist in the area of Peñasco Blanco.

Michael Marshall and others have observed that the two longest road segments—the North Road and the South Road—fix Chaco as a center place balanced halfway between north and south and between low and high places. The North Road consists of segments bearing true north, or within several degrees of true north, extending for more than thirty miles from Pueblo Alto, past Pierre's and Halfway House to Twin Angels at the edge of the Kutz Canyon badlands. Although erosion precludes ground verification, Stephen Lekson believes the road continued along Kutz Canyon to Salmon Ruin and then headed due north to Aztec. In contrast, I agree with Michael Marshall and Anna Sofaer that the road more likely was meant to terminate at Kutz Canyon, which represented a sacred subterranean space. Marshall points out that north is the direction of the *shipap*, or place of emergence, for Keres and Tewa peoples. In Keresan tradition, the souls of the dead return along a road to the north. The North Road could logically represent the invisible, the dead, and the subterranean. The South Road extends south-southwest for more than thirty miles from Chaco Canyon to the Dutton Plateau. Although it is unclear exactly where the road leaves the canyon (both Fajada Gap

Astronomical Alignments

The cardinal orientation north-south is a notable presence in Chacoan buildings such as Pueblo Bonito, Pueblo Alto, Tsin Kletsin, and Hungo Pavi. Great kivas are always oriented along a symmetrical north-south axis. Well-known, excavated examples include Casa Rinconada and the great kiva at Aztec West. The work of Anna Sofaer and others has demonstrated that astronomical orientations were another way the Chacoans represented themselves as the center—in this case, the center of celestial movements. The "sun dagger" petroglyph atop Fajada Butte tells us that Chacoans were interested

Figure 11.5. The gentle swale of the prehistoric Chacoan roadway known as the South Road, northeast of Kin Ya'a.

in solstices and equinoxes. Astronomical alignments also characterize some great houses. For example, the cardinal orientation of Pueblo Bonito showcases patterns of shadow and light that correspond to the equinox—the midpoint of the sun's journey on the horizon—reinforcing the position of this canyon great house as a center place within the larger universe as well as within Chacoan quotidian experience.

Sofaer's research suggests that the Chacoans were also interested in lunar standstills and that they oriented some architecture to emphasize the drama of these events. On the minor lunar standstill, for example, the full moon rises directly along the back wall of Chetro Ketl. At the outlier Chimney Rock, the major lunar standstill is framed between twin spires of rock. Sofaer believes these orientations were part of the conscious construction of Chaco Canyon as not only the topographic but also the celestial center of the universe, halfway between the movements of the sun and moon, at the midpoint between the future and the past.

Roads through Time

Some road segments position Chacoan buildings in time. The use of alignments to create "bridges

through time" was first recognized by John Stein and Andrew Fowler at post-Chacoan sites in Manuelito Canyon, near Gallup. I have described one such "bridge" at the outlier Red Willow, where a road segment links the late-eleventh-century great house with an isolated, tenth-century great kiva several miles away. The deliberate connection between two major structures separated by 150 years suggests that the road builders were making a conscious appeal to the past, constructing social memory for their own, late-eleventh-century purposes.

Another instance of alignment through time is found in Chaco Canyon, where two road segments lead northerly from Tsin Kletsin, the early-twelfth-century great house atop South Mesa. One segment points due north toward Pueblo Alto, a major eleventh-century edifice on the opposite side of the canyon, while the other extends slightly northwest toward New Alto, Pueblo Alto's early-twelfth-century neighbor. Standing atop Tsin Kletsin one pristine July morning, I realized that one purpose of these very deliberate alignments was to attach Tsin Kletsin by cardinal direction to the old, eleventh-century order of Pueblo Alto while at the same time creating a new, twelfth-century axis linking Tsin Kletsin with its contemporary, New Alto. Steve Lekson's "Chaco meridian"—a north-south connection between Chaco and the later sites of Aztec and Paquimé—is problematic in several respects but could be viewed as another case of a directional alignment reaching across time.

In all these ways, we can see the Chacoans constructing a sacred geography, playing with visibility, directionality, astronomical alignments, and temporal references to construct their world as the center place, at the nexus of space and time, at an intersection of horizontal and vertical planes. Chaco Canyon was an axis mundi for ancestral Pueblo

Figure 11.6. As part of the surveys of the 1970s, archaeologists examine a low stone wall edging an ancient road segment.

peoples. They built great houses, great kivas, roads, and shrines that emphasized balance among opposing forces such as north-south, up-down, visible-invisible, sun-moon, and summer-winter. When Chacoan people moved through the canyon or the surrounding landscape, they were actively reaffirming their beliefs about the nature of the world and their place in it.

Acknowledgments

I thank Randy McGuire for comments on an earlier version of this chapter. Many of the ideas presented here are based on the work of others, including especially Stephen Lekson, Michael Marshall, John Roney, Anna Sofaer, John Stein, Phillip Tuwaletstiwa, and Thomas Windes. I wish to acknowledge these researchers' intellectual contributions to the substance of the article. The ultimate interpretations presented in it are my own, however, and I take full responsibility for any misrepresentations or errors.

Ruth Van Dyke, an assistant professor of anthropology at Colorado College, is the author of numerous scholarly articles and a forthcoming book, *Lived Landscapes* (School of American Research Press). Her research interests focus on Chacoan outliers and landscape, particularly the use of experiential approaches to understanding Chaco.

Figure 12.1. The spiral petroglyph or "sun dagger" site on Fajada Butte, a solar and lunar calendrical marker.

Sacred Time in Chaco Canyon and Beyond

twelve

J. McKim Malville

In the calendars of the Western world, ordinary linear time outweighs sacred time, whereas in traditional cultures the opposite often holds true. Sacred days commemorate great and momentous events of the past. Because the earth keeps revolving around the sun, these days, such as the winter solstice, keep returning year after year. At these times the sacred seems to enter the ordinary world.

Ordinary time is marked by a linear sequence of similar days that fill the space between festivals and sacred days like colorless and odorless insulation. Western calendars give us linear time and enable us to count the days in order to anticipate the events of sacred time ("twelve days until Christmas"). The earliest known record of linear time was carved on a piece of eagle wing bone found in a cave in France's Dordogne Valley and dating to 30,000 BCE. A series of markings on the bone appears to record the day-to-day changing phases of the moon. The full moon appears some fifteen marks after the new moon. Because both full and new moon might have been viewed as powerful, this earliest of all calendars appears to have combined sacred and linear time.

Some twenty-five thousand years later, in the southern Sahara just west of Abul Simbel, nomadic pastoralists placed a calendar circle in the sand at the edge of a seasonal lake known as Nabta Playa. The circle contains sight lines that mark the direction of true north and the rising position of the sun at summer solstice. Summer monsoon rains moved northward to the Sahara around the time of the solstice, providing water for the lake. The rains that fell on the parched land would certainly have confirmed that summer solstice was a sacred time.

Closer to Chaco Canyon, in 1881 the army officer and amateur ethnologist John Bourke was able to examine a Zuni calendar stick carried by Nayuchi, head priest of the Bow clan. Bourke reported that Nayuchi's calendar stick consisted of three sets of ten marks of linear time, with occasional dots and signs to mark the ritual and festival days. Thirty days is close to the cycle of phases of the moon. Three weeks of ten days each would have been the Zuni month, which started with the full moon. The Zuni year started with an observation of the sun at winter solstice, followed by a ritual fire ceremony ten days later, indicated on the prayer stick by a circular burn mark. During the ten days between the solstice and the fire ceremony, no new fires were lighted and no one was allowed to leave the pueblo. The lighting of the new fire and its distribution were the powerful events that ended the old year and began the new.

The Chacoans, too, must have lived by a combination of sacred and ordinary time. The three-slab site near the top of Fajada Butte, with its nineteen-turn spiral petroglyph, is emblematic of the attention Chacoans paid to the cycles of the sun and moon. I know of no other place in the ancient world that combines so concisely the annual cycle of the sun and the 18.6-year standstill cycle of the moon. (The moon rises at a different point on the horizon every day, completing its movement from north to south and back again in about a month. The distance the moon travels in its monthly oscillation changes in a cycle of 18.6 years, the so-called standstill cycle.)

Figure 12.2. Equinox sunrise as observed from the Piedra Overlook site, Chimney Rock Archaeological Area, near Pagosa Springs, Colorado.

Chacoan astronomers were certainly among the world's most skillful in identifying the cycles of the sun and moon. The three-slab site is not a place for large public ceremonies. Its spiral petroglyphs are small and can be viewed by only a few people at one time. High above the floor of the canyon, the site seems a special and sacred place for celebrating major events in the lives of the sun and moon. The remnants of a ramp lead to the summit of Fajada Butte, a ramp that would have provided relatively easy access to astronomer-priests and other celebrants.

As is true in many traditional societies, Chacoans might have felt themselves closely connected to the cosmos and its rhythms. For them, the sun's cyclical return to December solstice might have been rich with meaning, a time for ceremonies that reenacted the events in which ancestors emerged from worlds beneath our own. The cosmos needed periodic regeneration, and such renewal might have involved not only periodic festivals in the canyon but also the extinguishing and rekindling of a ceremonial fire. One of the most dramatic places for such a fire would have been a great fire pit at the highest point of the high mesa on which Chimney Rock great

house is located. The message of that fire could have been passed southward to Pueblo Alto via the summit of Huérfano Mountain.

A symbolic center and axis of the Chacoan world, the canyon might also have been viewed as a *sipapu* that witnessed the emergence of the ancestors. As such, Chaco Canyon would have been an eminently appropriate place to celebrate the birth of the world at winter solstice. Pilgrims might have walked along roads that led inward to the center, filling the great houses during periodic festivals.

Time is both sacred and practical. It emerges mysteriously from the heavens and shares the power and sanctity of the dome of the heavens. One of humankind's great inventions, the calendar must have been developed independently many times throughout human history. The Chacoan calendar may have been an entirely local invention. A major difference between the jungles of Mexico, home of the Maya Indians, who devised an early and elaborate calendar, and the deserts and canyons of the Southwest is the latter's distant and sharp horizon on which to mark repetitive, cyclical events. With only trees on their horizon, the Mayas missed the phenomena of lunar standstills. They were, however, enthralled with Venus and Mars, an interest that seems not to have been transmitted to Chaco Canyon.

The horizon calendar was probably primarily a ritual or ceremonial device rather than an agricultural tool. In the San Juan Basin, year-to-year variations in soil moisture are too great for people to determine planting times only from the motion of the sun along the horizon. Dates of planting had to be established according to the experiences of on-the-spot farmers, not according to the abstract time of a calendar.

On the other hand, if one needed to get large numbers of people together from great distances for a

Figure 12.3. Chimney Rock great house looking toward Chaco Canyon.

ceremony, ritual, or festival, a precise calendar shared by the entire community was a necessity. The role of astronomy in pilgrimage festivals would have included identifying the nights of full moon, so that pilgrims walking into the canyon could benefit from moonlight in the evening. An accuracy of a few days would have been needed if everyone was to arrive at the same time. When travel of more than a week was involved, travelers needed to know when to leave home in order to avoid either wasting time waiting at the destination or missing the festival entirely. Long-distance signaling, such as that between Chimney Rock and Pueblo Alto, could have helped synchronize the calendars of various outlier communities.

Winter solstice, a time when the people and the land depended upon the sun's return north, has been an important calendrical event among the historic Pueblos. At Zuni, the winter solstice celebration is scheduled for the day of the closest full moon. A festival on such a day might have been at the core of sacred time in Chaco Canyon, a time when the beginning of the world was celebrated and reenacted.

Evidence of horizon calendars elsewhere in the Four Corners area reveals that ancestral Pueblo people took great interest in marking the cycles of time. Although they may not all have been contemporaneous, major markers for the winter solstice are found at Yucca House (where the winter solstice sun sets over the toe of Sleeping Ute Mountain) and at Cliff Palace at Mesa Verde (where the sun sets over the center of the Sun Temple). Summer solstice is precisely marked at Chimney Rock (where the sun rises along the north wall of the Chimney Rock great house), at Yellow Jacket (where sunrise is marked by a standing monolith), and at Hovenweep (where a horizontal spear of sunlight crosses a petroglyph panel near Holly House).

There is irony in the fact that within Chaco Canyon, few opportunities exist for making precise observations of the sun or moon on the horizon. As seen from most of the great houses, the natural horizon is too smooth to allow one to make direct calendrical determinations against it. Consequently, artificial calendrical devices may have been established

Figure 12.4. Corner window at Pueblo Bonito.

at places such as a corner window at Pueblo Bonito or the niche at Casa Rinconada, where a beam of sunlight thrown on an interior wall could have marked certain days. Both examples, however, are problematical in that exterior walls might have blocked the entry of light into the structure. The niche at Casa Rinconada might not even have been visible; a screen supported by small beams in the wall may have covered it. But the niche is visible today, and the movement of light into its center demonstrates to modern-day visitors the cyclical nature of time. Interior walls were generally plastered, and so calendrical markers could have been painted on the walls of great houses and great kivas to establish important dates. In such cases the calendrical devices would have been secondary, established only after appropriate dates had been obtained elsewhere by direct observations at a primary calendrical station.

A primary station needs an irregular horizon that enables precise determination of the position of the rising or setting sun at key points in time. It should be conveniently located close to a habitation for easy access by a keeper of the calendar, and it should provide an opportunity for both anticipation and confirmation of dates of festivals. Only after observing that the daily motion of the sun along the horizon had slowed, stopped, and then reversed direction could a Chacoan astronomer-priest have been certain that a solstice had occurred.

A spiral petroglyph on the northeast face of Piedra del Sol, near the Una Vida great house, provides that kind of certainty and may have been the primary source of dating for the carving of the spiral on Fajada Butte. Approximately two weeks before the summer solstice, a pyramidal rock some seventy meters northeast of Piedra del Sol casts its triangular shadow across the center of the spiral. Because of the shadow's penumbra, the position of the shadow on

Figure 12.5a. The shadow cast by the pyramidal rock across Piedra del Sol before the summer solstice.

Figure 12.5b. Sunrise in relation to the pyramidal rock on June 13.

the spiral petroglyph cannot be used as a precise day marker. However, an observer standing just in front of the center of the spiral can make precise direct observations of the sun on the horizon.

As viewed from this location, the sun rises over the top of the pyramidal rock on June 4–6, providing a countdown of fifteen to seventeen days until summer solstice. Prior to June 4–6, successive dawn suns climb the southern edge of the horizon pyramid, giving further opportunities for anticipation of solstice. For a few days around the solstice, the sun rises on a clearly identifiable notch to the north of the pyramid, enabling confirmation of the date. Piedra del Sol is directly visible from Fajada Butte, so information about the solstice could easily have been passed upward.

The great house known as Wijiji, built around 1110, is an excellent primary calendrical station for winter solstice. As viewed from the northwest corner of the house, the sun rises at the sharply defined northern edge of a notch on the southeastern horizon on December 4–5, thus offering a sixteen- to seventeen-day opportunity for precise anticipation of winter solstice. Confirmation of the solstice occurs when the sun reaches the southern edge of the notch. This site might have functioned as a calendrical station before the great house was built, and the calendrical activity might have been partly responsible for the particular location of this great house.

Another opportunity for anticipation and confirmation of winter solstice is found at the great house Kin Kletso, constructed between 1125 and 1130. Again, a sixteen- to seventeen-day opportunity for anticipation and confirmation of winter solstice begins when the sun rises at the base of the prominent cliff to the southeast. When viewed from the north wall of the great house, the sun appears at the base of the cliff on December 4–5. From the south wall, the rising sun appears at the base of the cliff on the solstice itself. The large boulder incorporated into the western portion of the building might have served as a sun-watching site before the great house was erected.

Ancestral Pueblo sky watchers observed not only the solstices but also the equinoxes. At the three-slab site on Fajada Butte, the days of the equinoxes are

Figure 12.6. The sun's southward movement along the horizon is apparent in this series of photographs made at sunrise on (from top to bottom) December 2, 6, and 15, from Wijiji in Chaco Canyon.

marked by a dagger of light that crosses a smaller secondary spiral. These days might also have been sacred events, especially the morning of the vernal equinox. The most precise timing of the equinoxes could have been accomplished at Chimney Rock, where the major site called Piedra Overlook (5AA8)

Figure 12.7. Major standstill moonrise at Chimney Rock.

was established exactly west of the gap between the chimneys. Residents of Piedra Overlook would have been greeted by glorious sunrises on the spring and fall equinoxes. Announcement of those sunrises could have been passed directly to Chimney Rock Pueblo and then down to Pueblo Alto via Huérfano Mountain.

Fajada Butte is a visual axis mundi. Its spire is a huge sundial casting a moving shadow across the floor of the canyon, thereby giving humans a means of measuring time. The length of its shadow grows, diminishes, and then grows again as the seasons come and go. The whole of time is collapsed onto the petroglyph panel near its summit, where the cycles of the earth, sun, and moon are marked by light and shadow.

Among the modern Pueblo Indians, universal harmony is maintained through correct and careful performance of rites and ceremonies at specific times of the year. Cyclical time puts one in touch with eternity, as time may seem to be collapsed to a point, "the still point of the turning world," to quote the poet T. S. Eliot.

The wholeness and depth of time become reachable in the periodic recurrence of astronomical events. Every dawn, the birth of the world may be experienced by watching and honoring the rising sun. Every winter solstice, the extended Chacoan community may have celebrated the beginning of time with ceremonies and dances. Perhaps the people of Chaco also participated in sacred lunar time, and every 18.6 years, when the moon's shadow touched the edge of the Fajada spiral and the moon rose between the spires of Chimney Rock, sacred time might again have been celebrated in the canyon and beyond.

J. McKim Malville, emeritus professor and former chair of the Department of Astrophysical and Planetary Sciences at the University of Colorado, taught astronomy there and studied numerous aspects of solar physics. He has long been interested in archaeoastronomy. His books include *Prehistoric Astronomy in the Southwest* and *Ancient Cities, Sacred Skies: Cosmic Geometries and City Planning in Ancient India*.

Understanding Chacoan Society

Lynne Sebastian

When I give lectures on the social and political organization of Chaco Canyon, people settle back in their chairs, ooh and aah over my slides, and wait expectantly for me to deliver The Truth About How It Was. They are disconcerted to learn that the answer is, "We don't know." We have ideas, theories, a huge number of bits and pieces of the puzzle, but no consensus yet about The Truth.

The problem, of course, is that we are talking about a set of abstract organizational principles—centralization, hierarchy, leadership, status, social groups, kin groups, and, most of all, social, political, and economic power. These principles underlie the basic relationships among people and groups that structure all human societies, but studying such relationships in the past, where all we have is the archaeological record, is much more complicated than studying, say, ceramic technology or trade.

Technology, trade, subsistence, and many of the other topics that archaeologists study leave direct, relatively unambiguous physical traces in the archaeological record. The organizational aspects of a society, however, have to be inferred from patterns in that record, and because our interpretations may be based on several levels of inference, they are subject to considerable debate. The very same patterns in the archaeological record may be offered as support for completely different interpretations.

This is exactly what has happened in the case of Chacoan society. After more than one hundred years of research, we know a great deal about the physical remains the Chacoan people left behind, and we are learning more all the time about the patterns that can be traced in those remains. Despite some differences of opinion, most Chaco scholars share the same basic understanding of the physical remains and the patterns. But when it comes to inferring the social and political structures that produced the patterning and the remains, disagreement abounds.

This is what is sometimes referred to as the difference between descriptive knowledge and explanatory knowledge. As the chapters in this book and the enormous quantity of scholarly literature demonstrate, we possess a great deal of descriptive knowledge about Chaco, and much of it offers clues to the way Chacoan society was organized. But archaeologists are still a long way from being able to piece those clues together into a coherent, unambiguous picture of the structure of that society.

Competing Views of Chacoan Organization

There are several schools of thought on the subject of Chacoan social and political organization, but they can, without too much unfairness, be lumped into two groups. One consists of those archaeologists who view Chacoan society as having exhibited substantial inequalities in social, political, and economic power, and the other represents those who think that the patterns in the Chacoan archaeological record can be accounted for without having to resort to schemes based on inequality. In the interest of full disclosure, I should say that I belong to the former group, but I will do my best to present both arguments here. Although I focus much of this discussion on Chaco Canyon and its immediate surroundings, many of the issues and concepts are germane to the larger Chaco world.

Figure 13.1. The massive walls, fine masonry, **T**-shaped doorways, and large rooms of Pueblo Bonito exemplify Chacoan great-house architecture.

Ancestral Pueblo pictograph panel on Chacra Mesa.

Peñasco Blanco great house, west end of Chaco Canyon.

Chaco Wash in a summer flood.

Petroglyphs along Chaco Wash near Wijiji.

Kivas in morning fog at Pueblo Bonito. This great house includes thirty-three kivas.

Pueblo del Arroyo in winter.

View of the central-western portion of Chaco Canyon, with Pueblo Bonito at bottom center and Pueblo del Arroyo immediately above it along Chaco Wash.

Chimney Rock great house in southern Colorado with the spires of Chimney Rock behind.

Those who interpret Chaco as having been organized around differential access to social, political, and economic power point to a number of patterns in the archaeological record to support their view. The architectural differences between great houses and small houses and the presence of a small number of rich burials in the great houses are offered as evidence of status differentiation. The Chacoans' ability to mobilize and organize substantial and complex labor efforts is attributed to the actions of powerful leaders. And the unified, apparently symbolic design of the buildings and landscape features in the central canyon by the end of the 1000s CE is offered as evidence for centralized planning and control.

Those who favor a more egalitarian form of organization, on the other hand, view the central canyon as a ceremonial center maintained by a cadre of priests and largely empty except during periodic influxes of pilgrims. As part of these ritual-based, calendrically organized events, materials were brought to the canyon or collected locally and used in cooperative construction efforts at the great houses. Leadership in these models is viewed as segmentary and situational rather than centralized and institutional.

As I discuss in more detail later, the central issues dividing these competing views of Chacoan society are the roles and definitions of things that are termed "ritual" and things that are termed "political." Those who view Chaco as a society marked by differences in social power acknowledge the central role of ritual both as the idiom within which power was expressed and as one of the bases of social and political power. Control of esoteric knowledge is so central to the power structure of modern Pueblo society that it would be surprising if such control were not a component of ancestral Pueblo societies as well. But those who interpret Chaco as a differentiated society consider ritual to have been a factor in the political structure, not a replacement for it.

Those who view Chaco as a "rituality" or the central canyon as a "location of high devotional expression" (see chapter 14), however, see Chacoan society as a religious phenomenon and not as a political one. They tend to equate "political" power with differential distribution of wealth and with a hierarchy whose apex is occupied by a single, self-aggrandizing individual—a chief or a king. Because they feel that there is little evidence in the archaeological record for either powerful individuals or inequitable distribution of wealth, they conclude that Chacoan society was not politically organized.

Why Is This So Hard?

Although one might expect disagreement about the details, one would think that archaeologists could at least come to a consensus about whether Chaco was a largely egalitarian enterprise or not. What is the problem here? In addition to the basic complexity of making inferential arguments about social organization at all, there are a number of reasons why this process is especially difficult in the Chacoan case. One of the problems is the absence of critical data—specifically, data related to the function of the great houses. A second problem, already noted, is an unfortunate tendency among archaeologists to dichotomize "ritual" and "political." Still another problem is that Southwestern archaeologists often have an unduly narrow perspective on what might be appropriate analogs for the organization of Chacoan society.

Problems of Data

The central issue on which most interpretive controversies about Chaco hinge is the function of the great houses. The canyon great houses have been envisioned as everything from enormous apartment buildings, palaces and barracks, and empty ceremonial structures to vast storehouses, elite residences, and a whole range of other, multifunctional things. Most, but not all, Chaco scholars have come to believe that some people lived in the great houses, but relatively few considering the immense size of these buildings. This interpretation is based on modern excavations at Pueblo Alto (which is atypical of canyon great houses in a number of ways) and sketchy information from late-nineteenth- and early-twentieth-century excavations at Pueblo Bonito and Chetro Ketl. These available data seem to show a paucity of domestic features and a preponderance of entirely featureless rooms.

Without some basis for estimating how many people lived in the canyon great houses, it is impossible to estimate the population of the canyon as a

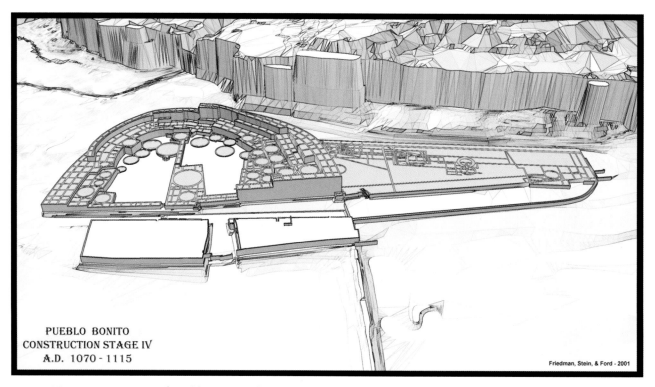

PUEBLO BONITO
CONSTRUCTION STAGE IV
A.D. 1070 - 1115

Friedman, Stein, & Ford - 2001

Figure 13.2. Reconstruction of Pueblo Bonito. The size and complexity of the great houses of downtown Chaco have stimulated a variety of interpretations regarding their possible functions.

whole. And population size is critical to any sociopolitical reconstruction because it tells us about availability of labor and about the relationship of population to the canyon's agricultural carrying capacity. Reliable population estimates are also important because worldwide studies have shown that there are consistent population thresholds that tend to trigger shifts in organizational complexity.

Even more critical, without modern excavation data to indicate the kinds and intensities of activities that took place in the great houses, we will never be able to understand the function(s) of these defining artifacts of Chacoan society. Although there are other important physical remains of the Chacoan world, from an archaeological perspective it is the great houses that define the extent of that world, both in space and in time. Some excavation is taking place at a small number of outlier great houses, and this is essential to our understanding of what the outliers were and how they related to the central canyon. Unfortunately, for reasons outside the control of the discipline of archaeology, new excavations in the canyon great houses are no longer possible and may not be possible for a very long time.

Given the currently available information, which is limited and probably not very representative, we can say that the canyon great houses had at least small resident populations but also contain a very large proportion of featureless rooms. We have evidence that some rooms were used to store religious paraphernalia and that some were used as crypts for repeated burials. Some of the burials in Pueblo Bonito, at least, contained large amounts of turquoise and other costly items. Perhaps most importantly, whatever function we may posit for the great houses—apartment buildings, storehouses, elite residences—they did not have to take on the monumental form that they did simply to fulfill those functions. We have to assume that their monumentality was an important function in its own right.

Detailed modern excavation data from one of the early canyon great houses are also critical if we are to understand the evolution of Chacoan society. However Chaco operated from 1030 to 1130, it did not start out with that full-blown set of power relationships. Chacoan society evolved gradually from the late 800s through the early 1000s and then quite suddenly underwent some extraordinary changes.

Figure 13.3. Peñasco Blanco, one of Chaco Canyon's three original great houses.

Among these changes were massive additions to the original great houses, which had stood nearly unchanged for more than one hundred years. If we could use archaeology to see what one of the original great houses—say, Peñasco Blanco or Una Vida—was and did during its first century and compare that with what it was and did during the so-called golden century, we would be in a much stronger position to understand the character and structure of Chacoan society.

Problems of Definition

The great divide between competing views of Chacoan society concerns the central organizing principle: was it "ritual" or "political"? In part this is a definitional issue. Those who deny that leadership in Chaco was "political" tend to define this term as meaning bureaucratic, administrative control exercised by individuals. They view "political" organization as being inherently secular and competitive, whereas ritual-based organization is envisioned as focusing on the sacred and expressing itself in com-

munal action. Political leaders, in this view, hold an office and benefit personally from that office, whereas ritual leaders maintain and pass on esoteric knowledge and perform a service for the common good.

In the opposing view, "political" refers simply to the web of relationships of social power that structures all human societies. And from that perspective, Chaco was unquestionably a political phenomenon. Almost no one denies that ritual activities and events were an extremely important component of Chacoan life; the Chacoans even transformed the physical world they inhabited into a highly designed, clearly symbolic landscape. And if the physical world was ordered by ritual, it is likely that most of the human experience was ordered by ritual as well. The pervasiveness of ritual in the Chacoan world does not, however, mean that the web of power relationships that we call "politics" was any less pervasive. One need only consider the history of medieval Europe or colonial Massachusetts or nineteenth-century Utah or the modern Middle East to find societies overtly ordered by the sacred and yet intensely political.

Political power can be based on many things. Control over critical economic resources is a common power base, as is control over the means of production and of marriages and alliance formations. Political power can be based on coercion through the control of physical force or through control of spiritual necessities and sacraments. Political power is simply the ability of one individual or group to control or constrain the actions of others.

One of the central tenets held by those who deny that Chaco was a political enterprise is that "political power" is equated with self-aggrandizing individuals and differential distribution of personal wealth. The argument is made that there is very little evidence in Chaco Canyon for differences in personal wealth; therefore there were no powerful individuals, and therefore Chaco was not politically organized or controlled.

The counterargument is that political power does not reside only in powerful individuals; it can be vested in corporate groups such as clans, lineages, fraternities, or councils. Chiefs and kings are not the only routes to political centralization and complexity. And any claim that there are no obvious differences in wealth in Chaco ignores one of the

defining features of "Chaconess." There were great houses and there were small sites, and some people lived in one and some people lived in the other. The great houses were enormously costly—in labor, in planning, in logistics, in the millions of building stones, in the intricate masonry, in the volume of water needed for even a small addition, and—perhaps most expensive of all—in the lavish use of wood in this nearly treeless environment. Some people in the canyon were living large (or great, actually), and some were not.

In addition, a few individuals were buried with rich arrays of grave goods in Pueblo Bonito. There are too few such burials to account for the entire political structure of Chacoan society, certainly, but there are some. Anywhere else in the world, these burials would be readily accepted as clear evidence of status differentiation. Any reconstruction of social roles and structure in Chaco has to account for these individuals and for the generally taller, healthier, more robust physical character of the burial populations from the great houses.

Problems of Analogy

As I have mentioned, we archaeologists observe patterns in the physical remains left behind by previous societies and offer interpretations about life in the past that account for those patterns. Virtually every interpretation we make is based, consciously or subliminally, on analogy with patterns observed in the modern world and with the cultural behaviors that created those patterns. In Southwestern archaeology we are both blessed and cursed by the continued presence of living descendants of the ancestral Pueblo people. These descendants have not only tenaciously survived but have, to a remarkable extent, been able to preserve knowledge of and substantial portions of their traditional lifeways.

This is a blessing because it provides us with the potential for detailed, clearly applicable analogies for a wide variety of past behaviors. It is a curse because the richness of the living cultures makes it too easy to grow myopic and not consider other cultural patterns from beyond this region.

One of the basic assumptions of archaeology is that physical patterns in the archaeological record reflect, in some way, organizational patterns in the

Figure 13.4. Human head from an effigy pottery vessel found at Pueblo Bonito.

Figure 13.5. Small sites such as 29SJ629 also are found in Chaco Canyon and may have housed the majority of the canyon's inhabitants.

living culture. The Chacoan archaeological record reflects a society that was physically organized very differently from the Pueblo villages as they were recorded after European contact. The great houses and small sites, great kivas, mounds, roads, earthworks, and constructed landscapes of Chaco Canyon have no real analogs in the Pueblo record after the mid-1200s. Despite this indication that Chaco is also likely to have been socially organized in a way very different from the ethnographically known pueblos, some archaeologists have been reluctant to abandon the Pueblo Indians as an analog for the social organization of Chacoan society.

Some researchers have adopted what seem to me rather tortuous scenarios to account for the highly differentiated physical remains of Chaco while retaining the communal, egalitarian, relatively undifferentiated social structure ascribed to the ethnographic Pueblos. Some scenarios involve enormous mobilizations of material and investments of labor in large, uniform additions to the great houses, all of which is described as having happened without centralized planning or administration. Other scenarios involve large influxes of pilgrims who arrive simultaneously in Chaco Canyon and organize themselves cooperatively to carry out great ritual events.

It is true that little evidence of powerful individuals has so far been found in the Chacoan archaeological record, but this does not mean that we must try to force Chaco into the procrustean model of an egalitarian, communal, undifferentiated society. The absence of powerful individuals, if indeed they are absent in this case, does not necessarily mean the absence of a highly differentiated political organization. Political power, especially in formative societies, can be an attribute of corporate groups as well as of individuals.

And though it is not true that there is "nothing new under the sun," totally new things in the human experience are, in fact, very rare. Whatever we posit as an organizational model for Chaco should have some analog in the known history of human societies, at least until we have exhausted and disproved the applicability of the available analogs. In our efforts to interpret Chaco, we need to expand our search for analogs more widely, perhaps especially to Africa, where formative societies with politically powerful but corporate forms of leadership were relatively common.

Conclusion

If Chaco fit neatly into some straightforward organizational "box" based on common patterns that we see in the modern or historical world, we would have found that box by now. This does not mean that Chaco was some unique specimen never seen in the world before or since; that is theoretically possible but statistically unlikely. What is more likely is that we haven't looked at enough boxes yet. The extraordinary archaeological record of this society indicates both a strong political structure and an intense emphasis on ritual. Rather than focus on oppositions such as ritual versus political, we need to accept that Chacoan society included both and explore the nature of the relationships between ritual knowledge and authority and the distribution of social, political, and economic power.

Lynne Sebastian is director of historic preservation programs at the SRI Foundation and president of the Society for American Archaeology (2003–5). A specialist in the archaeology of the American Southwest, she is the author of *The Chaco Anasazi: Sociopolitical Evolution in the Prehistoric Southwest*.

Figure 14.1. The Stones of Stenness, a ceremonial site in the Orkney Islands.

fourteen

Chaco Canyon

A View from the Outside

Colin Renfrew

We in the ages lying
In the buried dust of the earth,
Built Nineveh with our sighing,
And Babel itself in our mirth;
And o'erthrew them with prophesying
To the old of the new world's worth:
For each age is a dream that is dying,
Or one that is coming to birth.

Arthur O'Shaughnessy, "Ode," 1874

During more than a century of archaeological research, scholars have offered varying perspectives on Chaco Canyon and the Chaco "phenomenon." One view, which I develop here, regards Chaco as an essentially egalitarian society whose economy was inextricably linked to its role as a ritual center. It is evident that the great kivas and great houses whose remains still impress visitors were actuated by a powerful and coherent belief system, responsible also for the "roads," or ceremonial promenades. In the eleventh and twelfth centuries, Chaco became a magnet for periodic religious pilgrimages—as such, I would call it a "location of high devotional expression."

The ode whose third and final verse is quoted above begins: "We are the music makers, / And we are the dreamers of dreams." Its somewhat "idealistic" view of material culture may be relevant in Chaco's case, as it is in several others. My approach to Chaco is colored by my experience of several other early societies that were by no means urban but that nonetheless boasted impressive monumental constructions and presumably symbolic features. Prominent among these parallels to Chaco are the so-called temples of prehistoric Malta; the *image ahu*, or statue shrines, of Easter Island; the Ring of Brogar and Stones of Stenness in the Orkney Islands of Scotland; the medieval pilgrimages made to the Church of St. James of Compostela in northern Spain and to other pilgrimage centers of the Roman Catholic Church; and the Olympic games (and other periodic games) of classical Greece.

The second verse of the poem makes a point that is worth emphasizing here, although at first sight it seems indeed romantic. Its line of thought leads us toward a preliminary conclusion that may prove useful:

With wonderful deathless ditties

We build up the world's great cities

And out of a fabulous story

We fashion an empire's glory;

One man with a dream, at pleasure,

Shall go forth and conquer a crown;

And three with a new song's measure

Can trample a kingdom down.

The conclusion is that there are some archaeological sites that we can begin to make intelligible to ourselves only if we regard them as the product of a powerful, imaginative symbolic system—a "dream." Implied here is a vision, worldview, or cognitive system of which we have at first sight no very clear idea. Our first task, then, is to press this view into a more explicitly anthropological terminology, so that the insight contained in O'Shaughnessy's words is not dismissed as mere poetic fancy.

From time to time archaeologists are confronted with the need to explain human products that seem to go well beyond needs that they themselves might consider "rational." Such products might be great monumental constructions, plazas and other open spaces of considerable scale, and the conspicuous consumption of material goods, perhaps evidenced by large finds of evidently high-value goods deposited and abandoned at a particular place.

Into the category of great monumental constructions would fall the *henge* monuments of the British Isles, including Stonehenge and the Orcadian henges. There would likewise fall the pyramids of Egypt. The conspicuous consumption of material goods would include "offerings" found at Greek temples—for instance, at Olympia—and spectacular grave goods accompanying rich burials. The open spaces would include the plazas at many Mesoamerican sites. In each case a prodigious amount of labor or valuable goods has been

Figure 14.2. Paving along a roadway connecting Pueblo Bonito and Pueblo del Arroyo to Pueblo Alto.

expended in order to achieve an effect that, although impressive, has little evident utilitarian purpose (other than to impress). But whereas some of these special sites are found in systems that display prominent social ranking, there are others, such as Stonehenge, the Maltese temples, and Chaco Canyon itself, for which the converse seems to be the case.

Costly and expressive acts such as these are frequently, though not always, manifestations of a powerful belief system. They usually also suggest a religion and often a belief in supernatural beings.

Locations of high devotional expression very often display monumental architecture. They often involve special approaches—constructions that regulate the manner in which they are approached and perhaps exclude or restrict certain areas. Their architects made use of what might be called "attention-focusing devices" that contain features, axes, and orientations of cosmological significance. In many cases they served as, or were accompanied by, gathering places in which, it may often be inferred, rituals were performed. Such rituals might have involved special equipment and been governed by formal rules. Often such locations are accompanied by expressive symbols on a large scale and abundant smaller symbols; iconic redundancy is a frequent feature.

Part of the material culture associated with such locations usually served to facilitate ritual, with the use of means to engage the senses—fire, light, musical instruments, foodstuffs, beverages (sometimes hallucinatory), perfumes, and so forth. Rich materials might also have been deliberately brought to the location from a wide range of places and left there as what we sometimes call offerings. Often there is evidence for the conspicuous consumption of food and drink; most "sacrifices" fall within this category. Other "sacrifices," including human ones, may be involved even in the absence of eating and drinking. Depending upon the context, these may be regarded as conspicuous consumption or offerings or both.

Major ritual centers often give indications of the presence of large numbers of people who came to witness or participate in the ceremonies or observances that took place. Such periodic assemblies inevitably had a range of functions. Visitors enjoyed social intercourse, exchanged information, and bartered in the markets. Men and women of marriageable age found opportunities to meet a mate.

Often such sites are not entirely exclusive and unique. It is common for larger and more monumental centers to be separated by smaller-scale centers of comparable form throughout a region. Gatherings there generally took place at well-determined time intervals, perhaps on occasions of calendrical significance. Annual periodicity was common, although the games of ancient Greece were held every two to four years.

One other interesting feature is worth stressing. In many cases, major ritual centers are found in circumstances in which either a large population would not have been predicted or a labor input on so large a scale by an established rural population might not have been expected. Indeed, they are sometimes located in isolated places where the limitations of steady supplies necessary for subsistence might result in stress. Chaco Canyon and the Orkney Islands certainly are isolated, as are Easter Island and Malta. Indeed, the very isolation and resulting privacy of these ritual sites might have contributed to the intensity of their emerging belief systems.

Chaco as a Location of High Devotional Expression

The obvious suggestion is that Chaco Canyon falls into the category of a location of high devotional expression. The monumental scale and symbolic aspects of its architecture and the presence of "roads" there support the suggestion. Countering the hypothesis are the absence of any wealth of iconography and the paucity of rich deposits of offerings. Indeed, at first sight, if ritual activity devoted to specific divinities took place at Chaco, then these were supernatural beings reticent in their personal iconography.

The focus for a location of high devotional expression, however, does not have to be primarily religious. Other devotional systems are possible, involving either loyalty to specific persons such as a chief or even loyalty to the group. Certainly, if one maintains that Chacoan great houses constituted perfectly ordinary residential complexes, then Chaco's status as a location of high devotional expression could be questioned. But their special features, the role of Chaco Canyon as the major focus of a region, and the suggestion that the number of persons resident in the great houses was much smaller than

Figure 14.3. The prehistoric Temple of Mnajdra on Malta.

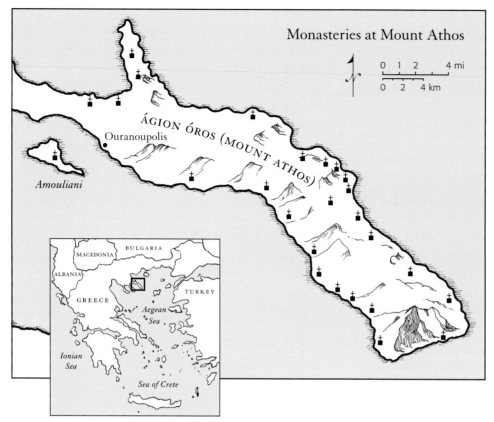

Figure 14.4.

their scale might at first suggest may be taken as arguments favoring the hypothesis.

Most locations of high devotional expression involve the presence of two or three types of people. First, there are pilgrims, who arrive periodically to attend the ceremonies that are the special activities of such sites. In the case of Chaco, one wonders from where the pilgrims came, how the pilgrimages were structured, and what type of regional organization was involved. Second, there is a resident population, which includes specialists such as priests and food preparers along with farmers maintaining their own way of life. Third, a high-status class possessing secular power may also be present. From the evidence at hand, it seems likely that the Chaco region functioned in terms of religious faith rather than under a centralized hierarchy of persons and an ideology of power.

Perhaps the most puzzling feature about Chaco Canyon is that at first it looks not like one major center but like several sites. Each of the largest great houses has its own great kiva, so that the architectural pattern takes on a modular aspect. We could

well imagine that Chaco acted as a pilgrimage center, with each great house serving as the *xenona* (Greek for "guesthouse" or "inn") and ceremonial focus for its own subregion within the region as a whole. It may be that the positioning of the "roads" could help in evaluating such a hypothesis.

We need to ask whether the canyon as a single site is correctly to be regarded as "modular," with each great house duplicating the function of its neighbors, each for a different subregion. Alternatively, we must ask whether it should be seen as consisting of specialized units, with a single focal and primary center (perhaps Pueblo Bonito) and others that might have fulfilled ancillary specialist roles.

It may be relevant that there are, elsewhere in the world, cases in which several religious and residential centers are or were situated within a major sacred center, each having a relationship with more distant hinterlands. A number of the Greek Orthodox monasteries at the great religious center of Mount Athos in Greece are each occupied by monks originating from a particular country to the north—Serbia and Bulgaria, for example. On a smaller scale, two of the great religious centers of ancient Greece, Delphi and Olympia—both places where periodic games were held—featured "treasuries" within the sacred *temenos* (precinct) that were the works of individual city-states that competed in the games.

To shift the focus from the sacred to the educational, there exist today in the Western world university centers whose colleges function as autonomous peer institutions (or modules) and have transient populations of three or four years' duration. They provide shelter and subsistence in exchange for payment, and they accept fees and benefactions. I do not seriously offer Cambridge as a paradigm for Chaco, or Trinity College as the counterpart of Pueblo Bonito. But we can see inevitable analogies in the economic organization of institutions of equivalent status that are grouped within the same major center, even when one case involves educational houses operating within a money economy, and the other, ritually focused great houses operating within a largely egalitarian society through the mechanism of redistribution.

Economic Considerations: Sacred and Profane

I should stress that I propose regarding Chaco Canyon as a location of high devotional expression not as a solution to a problem but rather as a means of investigating it. Consider, for example, the question of the economy of such a sacred place.

Within a religious context, large numbers of pilgrims import and consume goods. They also exchange goods with the site's year-round residents, who may provide them with part of their subsistence. The locals engage in farming, foraging, craft production, and other daily economic tasks, and they exchange goods with other communities. They also operate periodic markets for the benefit of pilgrims. There, pilgrims may acquire sanctified, locally made or imported objects to take home with them as souvenirs. An additional dimension of the economy may be the distribution of food or other resources by members of the central authority.

At the nub of the sacred economy is a special exchange transaction. The devotee comes to the ritual center and observes or takes part in special ceremonies. Thereby he discharges an obligation and receives the benefits of spiritual enlightenment or religious experience, or perhaps just simple entertainment. In return, he may be obliged to proffer tithes to the officiating priest in the form of foodstuffs and other materials, pay tribute to a secular authority in the form of labor on monumental constructions, or make benefactions of value to the presiding deity, spirit, or other sacred entity. These acts result in a substantial inflow of material goods or labor services. In the case of Chaco, an apparent increase in the utilization (and perhaps intentional

Figure 14.5. Pilgrims to Chaco Canyon might have brought objects such as these cylinder jars, uncovered at Pueblo Bonito, as gifts or religious offerings.

Figure 14.6. Bonito phase pitcher.

breakage) of pottery at Pueblo Alto might be a substantive reflection of these economic patterns. Moreover, Pueblo Alto's trash deposits appear to be layered in the mounds as if trash were deposited intermittently rather than daily.

These economies operate simultaneously and are not always easy to distinguish in the archaeological record. Not necessarily dependent upon hierarchical social order, they operate as effectively in an egalitarian society as in a chiefdom. Indeed, the concept of a location of high devotional expression does not distinguish between ritual centers that lack any coherent organizing capacity at the center and those that function within a highly ordered chiefdom or state society. Nevertheless, it is possible for major religious and pilgrimage centers to be egalitarian. And the concept of "redistribution" becomes a rather special one in which the incoming resource takes the form of material goods or labor while the counterpart of the exchange (other than in the case of a few outgoing sanctified objects) is entirely non-material. It consists of the religious experience and

the accompanying social experience for the individual of participating in a great seasonal fair. For the archaeologist, this benefit to the individual leaves little direct material trace. But at Chaco, its consequences are widely seen in the manner in which the great houses lying outside Chaco Canyon but within its region are, in their plans and architecture, recognizably the products of the "dream" periodically experienced by pilgrims at the center.

Colin Renfrew is Disney Professor of Archaeology and director of the McDonald Institute for Archaeological Research at the University of Cambridge. Books by Professor Lord Renfrew include *Before Civilization: The Radiocarbon Revolution and Prehistoric Europe*; *The Prehistory of Orkney*; and *Archaeology and Language: The Puzzle of Indo-European Origins*. This cahpter is adapted from "Production and Consumption in a Sacred Economy," reproduced by permission of the Society for American Archaeology from *American Antiquity* 66:1 (2001).

The Mesa Verde Region
Chaco's Northern Neighbor
William D. Lipe

In public perceptions of Southwestern archaeology, two images compete for attention—Pueblo Bonito, its massive masonry walls rising above the floor of Chaco Canyon in New Mexico, and Cliff Palace, its many rooms clustered under the canyon rim at Mesa Verde in Colorado. Both of these iconic sites are in the drainage basin of the San Juan River, an area of more than thirty thousand square miles that nurtured the growth and florescence of early Puebloan culture between about 500 and 1300 CE. Chaco Canyon is located on one of the southern tributaries of the San Juan, whereas the Mesa Verde culture area occupies the northern part of the drainage basin, extending across parts of southwestern Colorado, northeastern New Mexico, and southeastern Utah. This area has large tracts of wind-deposited soil that can be productively dry-farmed (that is, watered by direct rainfall alone). The Pueblo communities of the Mesa Verde region knew about, interacted with, and were affected by the growth and decline of the major Chacoan centers at Chaco Canyon and, later, Aztec.

Maize, that great promoter of Native American population growth, was introduced to the Mesa Verde region by the late centuries BCE, but population didn't "boom" until the 600s CE, in the late Basketmaker III period. At that time, small communities composed of scattered, one- or two-family farmsteads flourished in many parts of the region. People lived in large pithouses.

Between 750 and 900 CE—the Pueblo I period—Pueblo families in the greater San Juan River basin built more extensive dwellings, each consisting of a large pithouse, or "protokiva," used for cooking, sleeping, and rituals, and, just to the north, a small cluster of adjoined surface rooms that provided additional living and storage space. This basic arrangement persisted in the San Juan region through the end of the Pueblo III period in the late 1200s. Another persistent architectural form that was present by the 700s was the much larger "great kiva." Members of a number of families must have collaborated in the construction of great kivas. People used them for community gatherings—undoubtedly often involving religious ceremonies—that reinforced cooperation and a sense of shared identity.

During the Pueblo I period, the inhabitants of some parts of the Mesa Verde region moved from dispersed farmsteads into settlements of up to several hundred people. A few of their larger villages included one or two architecturally distinctive U-shaped roomblocks that had an "oversized" protokiva with especially elaborate ritual features (such as large vaults built into the floor on each side of a central fire pit). Evidence from excavations near Dolores, Colorado, suggests that families living in these special roomblocks probably gained status and political influence by hosting ceremonies and feasts.

Population began to decline in the Mesa Verde region at the very end of the 800s and remained small through the 900s (the early Pueblo II period). A severe drought that affected dry farming apparently contributed to the decline. Concurrently, population seems to have been growing in the southern San Juan River basin, where farming typically depended on

Figure 15.1. Cliff Palace in Mesa Verde National Park, the Southwest's largest cliff dwelling.

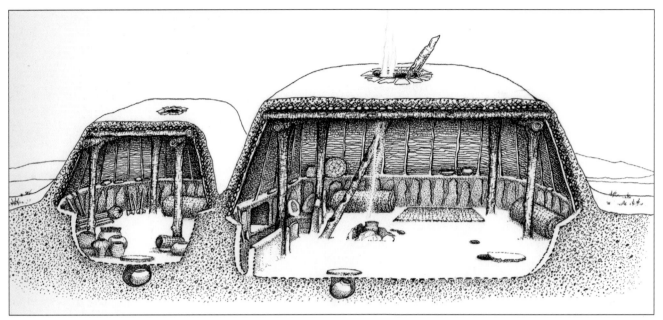

Figure 15.2. Reconstruction of a Basketmaker III pithouse in the northern San Juan region, showing an antechamber used to store household supplies and tools.

water from periodic floods in stream valleys or runoff from slopes. Evidence from pottery styles has enabled Richard Wilshusen and Scott Ortman to trace the migration of some groups from southwestern Colorado to new homes south of the San Juan (see chapter 3). This was also a time of population growth at Chaco Canyon. Construction at Pueblo Bonito and other early great houses followed a U-shaped plan perhaps derived from the special roomblocks at the earlier Pueblo I villages of the Mesa Verde region.

Chacoan Great Houses in the North

In the middle and late 1000s, population built up again north of the San Juan. Dispersed communities of scattered one- or two-family farmsteads were once again the norm. Each family had its own small kiva and set of surface living and storage rooms. Between about 1075 and 1130 (the late Pueblo II period), a number of communities built great houses with obvious architectural connections to Chaco Canyon. These include the Chimney Rock, Wallace, Escalante, Porter, and Lowry sites in Colorado, the Bluff great house in southeastern Utah, and the very large centers of Salmon and Aztec in the "Totah" region. The Totah—the word means "rivers come together" in Navajo—is the area of northwestern New Mexico surrounding the confluences of the Animas, La Plata,

and San Juan Rivers (see map, p. xii). This well-watered area was a focus of population and social development during the Pueblo II and Pueblo III periods.

In size and elaboration, Salmon and Aztec West rival the major great houses in Chaco Canyon, where new construction was winding down at this time. As at Chaco, well-organized teams built these large, multistory buildings in several episodes of intense effort. Tree-ring dating tells us that the builders of the Salmon great house, near Farmington, New Mexico, did most of their construction in 1088–90, 1093–94, and 1105–6. The even more massive building at Aztec West was largely built in two bursts of activity between 1112 and 1125. Many of the construction beams were spruce, fir, or pine logs carried from highlands thirty or more miles away.

Aztec West is the most imposing building in a much larger site complex, much of which remains unexcavated. This group of sites, which extends along the bluffs above the Animas Valley for more than a mile, contains many structures that appear to date to the early 1100s. A convincing case can be made that in the early 1100s, the seat of Chacoan religious and political power had moved to Aztec. (The site's name reflects erroneous nineteenth-century beliefs about connections between the

Figure 15.3. Salmon Ruin, a major Chacoan great house on the north bank of the San Juan River, was excavated in the 1970s and today has a visitors' center and museum.

they can be seen from a considerable distance. On the other hand, floor plans and modes of construction vary considerably from one great house to the next. My interpretation is that they were built under the direction of local leaders to serve as their residences and also as the religious and political centers of their respective communities. These leaders must have gained influence at home by associating themselves with the politico-religious elite of Aztec or perhaps even Chaco Canyon. They probably gained spiritual power and local respect by participating in ceremonies at one of these major centers and by making contributions of food, timbers, other goods, or labor as part of the visit. It seems reasonable to call these visits pilgrimages.

The Chimney Rock, Escalante, and Lowry great houses have been excavated and stabilized and are open to the public. Chimney Rock Pueblo, located near Pagosa Springs, Colorado, and managed by the US Forest Service, lies at seventy-six hundred feet in elevation on the narrow spine of a mesa overlooking the southern Rockies and the high valleys of the upper Piedra River drainage. Two closely spaced rock pinnacles at the end of the mesa give the site its name. Chimney Rock Pueblo consists of a compact roomblock of thirty-five ground-floor rooms with two large, blocked-in kivas. Portions of the building were probably two stories high. Tree-ring dates indicate that building took place in two episodes—in 1076 and 1093 CE. The archaeoastronomer J. McKim Malville has pointed out that these dates correspond to major lunar standstills and that at these times, a person standing close to the pueblo would have seen the moon rise between the twin pinnacles of Chimney Rock (see chapter 12).

Puebloan culture of the Four Corners area and the Aztec empire of central Mexico.)

The other Mesa Verde–region great houses, centered in existing communities of scattered farmsteads and hamlets, are much smaller than Aztec West and Salmon Ruin. Built with locally available stone and timbers, they are distinctive not so much for their size but because their architecture contrasts strongly in formality, elaboration, and positioning with the architecture of the surrounding residences. And unlike the ordinary residences, they usually were built in one or a few construction episodes instead of growing gradually as families needed additional rooms.

Typically, these small great houses are multistoried, with large rooms, blocked-in kivas (built within the surface roomblock), and thick, well-constructed masonry walls. They usually are associated with a masonry-lined great kiva with elaborate floor features, and often they are situated so that

One of the most striking aspects of Chimney Rock Pueblo is the contrast between its formal, very Chaco-esque architecture and that of the structures housing the surrounding community. Dubbed

Figure 15.4. A portion of Lowry Ruin.

"crater houses" by their excavator, Frank Eddy, these are essentially aboveground pithouses with extremely thick (three to five feet) rubble masonry walls.

Lowry Ruin, managed by the Bureau of Land Management and located northwest of Cortez, Colorado, was excavated in the 1930s by the archaeologist Paul Martin of the Field Museum in Chicago. The great house is a small but massive masonry roomblock with a nearby Chaco-style great kiva. Tree-ring dates indicate construction in 1085–1090, with additional building between 1106 and 1120. The domestic architecture of the surrounding community was very much in the Mesa Verde regional tradition. Also unlike Chimney Rock, the Lowry

great house continued to be used and remodeled perhaps into the 1200s.

Escalante Ruin, located near Dolores, Colorado, is adjacent to the Bureau of Land Management's Anasazi Heritage Center, a public museum and collections repository. Small even by southwestern Colorado standards, it stood only one story high and had twenty-five rooms with one blocked-in kiva. It is also the latest of the Mesa Verde– region great houses: tree-ring and pottery data indicate construction in the late 1120s and 1130s. There is no associated great kiva.

At this writing, Crow Canyon Archaeological Center is conducting research on the Albert Porter Pueblo northwest of Cortez, and the University of Colorado is working at the Bluff great house on the outskirts of Bluff, Utah, in the San Juan River valley. Catherine Cameron has documented an earthen berm surrounding the Bluff great house—a feature shared with many of the great houses at Chaco Canyon and elsewhere in the southern San Juan region. Both the Bluff and Porter great houses show extensive evidence of remodeling and occupation into the late 1100s and early 1200s; they evidently continued to be important buildings in their respective communities.

During the period of strong Chacoan (or perhaps I should say Aztecan) influence, from about 1075 to 1130, people in the Mesa Verde region frequently were able to trade for pottery and marine shell ornaments from outside the region. Even a few cast copper items—probably transported from western Mexico along Chacoan trade routes—have been found at sites in Colorado and Utah. People, goods, and ideas appear to have moved more freely and widely across the northern Southwest than they did either before or after this brief era. Ceremonies held at the major centers in Chaco Canyon and the Totah, and the attendant religious pilgrimages, likely promoted such interregional connections.

The biological anthropologist Christy G. Turner II and his wife and coauthor, Jacqueline A. Turner, in their book *Man Corn: Cannibalism and Violence in the American Southwest* (University of Utah Press, 1999), present an alternative view of the sources of Chacoan influence and power. They argue that political leaders at the major Chacoan centers used occasional acts of extreme violence and even cannibalism to extend and enforce their control over outlying areas. This hypothesis implies that in the Mesa Verde region, archaeological evidence of violence should coincide with the expansion and consolidation of the Chacoan great-house system between 1075 and 1130 CE.

Instead, the best-studied cases of extreme violence and cannibalism (from several sites near Cortez, Colorado) are dated between about 1130 and 1160, when the Chacoan great-house system appears to have been in decline. These years were, however, the first decades of a severe drought that lasted until about 1180. Before this, the Chacoan system seems to have promoted stable local leadership and peaceful relationships among communities. In contrast, the weakening and eventual breakdown of Chacoan influence, perhaps a result of the onset of the mid-1100s drought, might have allowed suppressed intra- and intercommunity conflicts to

surface. Social instability was likely exacerbated in some areas by localized food shortages resulting from the drought.

The archaeological record for the middle 1100s (the early Pueblo III period) in the Mesa Verde region is sparse and hard to interpret. Although the region was not abandoned, population probably declined, and most families and communities were "hunkered down" trying to get through the drought. Construction beams dating to the 1150s through the 1180s are particularly rare, indicating that few structures were built during those decades. The excavators of the great Chacoan centers of Aztec West and Salmon Ruin interpreted the evidence as indicating that these sites were largely vacant during the middle 1100s. Recent compilations of tree-ring dates from limited excavations at Aztec East—another major great house located adjacent to Aztec West—indicate that construction did continue there at a low level during these years. Some of the smaller habitation sites in the Aztec group probably also date to the middle and late 1100s, indicating that the locality continued to be populated at some level.

The tree-ring data from the Aztec complex and from Salmon Ruin also document a significant shift in the source of construction timbers after 1130. Thousands of ponderosa pine, spruce, and fir beams had been imported from distant mountains for the massive construction effort at Aztec West in the early 1100s. After the mid-1130s, people relied much more heavily on local juniper for the continuing construction at Aztec East. This implies that the systems for cutting and transporting large beams had broken down at Aztec after flourishing for only a few decades. A burst of building activity at Salmon in the late 1200s, however, included much juniper but also a few large conifer beams imported from a substantial distance, indicating that such efforts could still be organized on occasion. In general, though, the long-distance movement of goods seems to have declined in the Mesa Verde

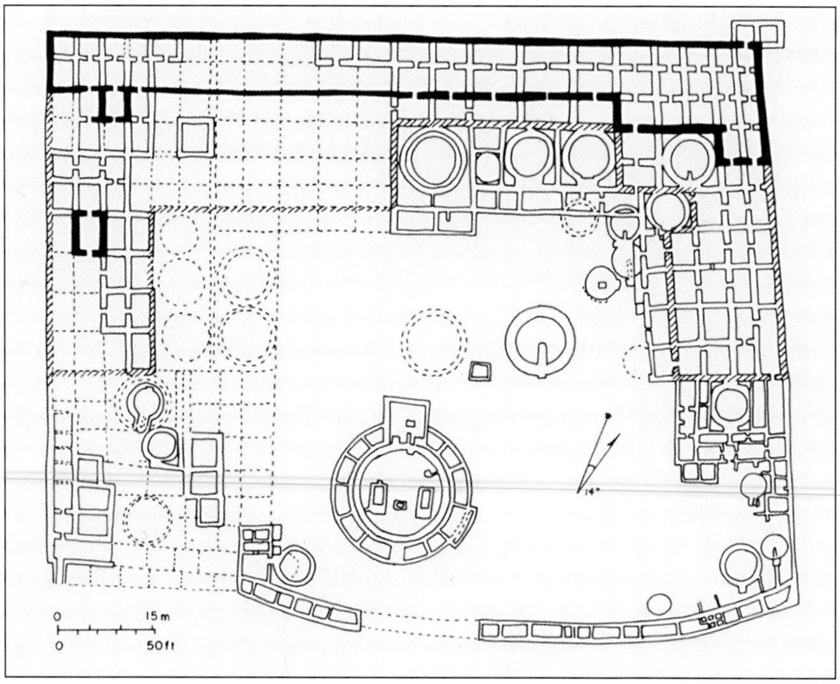

Figure 15.5. Plan of Aztec West, which had an estimated 405 rooms and 28 kivas.

area after the early 1100s. Items such as turquoise, shell, obsidian, and pottery from other parts of the Southwest appear less frequently in sites dating to the late 1100s and 1200s. Perhaps as the great Chacoan centers declined, the major religious ceremonies and the long-distance movement of people and goods they had fostered declined as well.

By the end of the 1100s, population was growing again throughout the Mesa Verde region, and the tree-ring record indicates that construction boomed as well. Most people continued to live in communities of dispersed farmsteads located close to their fields, but increasingly, communities of the early 1200s were centered on small villages housing a number of families. In some of these central villages, newly constructed two-story buildings stand out as the probable residences of leading families. The architectural contrasts between these buildings and surrounding ordinary residences are much more subtle than they were during the heyday of Chacoan great houses in the late 1000s and early 1100s.

Most of the Chacoan-era great houses in Colorado and Utah, as well as in the Totah region of New Mexico, saw renewed use during the 1200s. Many were remodeled by subdividing the large Chacoan-era rooms and inserting small Mesa Verde–style kivas into unused rooms. The changes seem designed to adapt the structures to residential use by numerous families, rather than to restore the great houses' architectural distinctiveness, formality, and exclusiveness. In some cases—especially in the Totah region—the great houses remained at the centers of their communities, but elsewhere these buildings frequently became peripheral as settlement locations shifted. Nonetheless, it seems likely that people recognized the symbolic importance of these Chacoan great houses, and they—or the people who lived in them—may have continued to play a role in the ceremonial life of their communities.

During the middle and late 1200s (late Pueblo III), large numbers of people occupied Salmon Ruin and the Aztec complex, confirming that these buildings continued to be politically and ceremonially central to their communities. Elsewhere in the Mesa Verde region, people increasingly moved to new kinds of sites in new locations on canyon rims, usually close to good springs. In areas where natural shelters were large and numerous, as on the Mesa Verde, cliff dwellings flourished—this was the time when Cliff Palace, Spruce Tree House, and the other well-known sites of Mesa Verde National Park reached their greatest size. Where natural shelters were unavailable, large villages such as Sand Canyon Pueblo, west of Cortez, were built in the open on the edges of canyons.

Novel architectural features and layouts characterized these late Pueblo III villages in Colorado and Utah. Although towers were present at a few sites in the 1100s, they became much more common at the canyon-oriented sites of the middle and late 1200s. This was especially so near the Utah-Colorado border, where good examples are preserved in Hovenweep National Monument. Also present at many of the canyon rim villages are large **D**-shaped structures with interior courtyards and peripheral storage structures; masonry walls surrounding all or part of the settlement; open plaza areas; and a bilateral layout in which two parts of the site were separated by a natural drainage or, in a few cases, a constructed wall. In location and architectural patterning, the late Pueblo III canyon-oriented villages of Colorado and Utah seem not to have been modeled on the Chacoan-era buildings at the Aztec center, even though these continued to be occupied. The bulk of evidence indicates that Aztec's influence over the larger Mesa Verde region continued to decline throughout the Pueblo III period.

Warfare intensified among the ancestral Puebloans of the Mesa Verde region during the late 1200s. We see evidence of this in the clustering of people into villages that are situated in defensible settings and have defensive features such as site-enclosing walls and towers. In addition, archaeologists have found human remains showing traces of violence. Recently, researchers were stunned to discover that in the late 1270s, an attack killed most or all of the residents of a small village west of present-day Cortez, a village known as the Castle Rock site.

In the Totah region, the old Chacoan great houses at Aztec West and Salmon and the "new" great house at Aztec East were in heavy use until the regional depopulation of the 1270s and 1280s. Their inhabitants were not immune to the cycle of violence that was playing out in the larger Mesa Verde region.

Figure 15.6. Holly Group, Hovenweep National Monument.

influence in the Mesa Verde region may have removed or weakened the previous ceremonial and economic ties that promoted peaceful relations among that area's communities and opened the door to escalating hostilities.

Climatic fluctuations must also have promoted conflict during the late Pueblo III period. Researchers at the Laboratory of Tree-Ring Research at the University of Arizona have discovered that summer rains—vital for both dry farming and runoff farming—became less reliable after about 1250. The early years of the "great drought" of 1276 to 1299 coincide almost perfectly with the rapid final depopulation of the Mesa Verde region. Although the regional population had declined somewhat after its peak in the early 1200s, thousands of people still occupied the Mesa Verde region as late as 1270. By sometime in the 1280s, however, a combination of emigration and in-place population decline had emptied the area of its ancestral

In the late 1260s or 1270s, a tragedy occurred at Salmon Ruin. Its tower kiva, located centrally in the great house, was burned, incinerating the bodies of forty-five to fifty-five individuals—many of them children—that had been placed on the roof prior to the conflagration.

Although Southwestern archaeologists once postulated that the Mesa Verde Puebloans were driven out by the ancestors of the Navajos or the Utes during Pueblo III times, they now believe that these peoples did not move into the area until later. It is likely that hostilities broke out sporadically among the Puebloan communities, with cycles of revenge and retribution escalating the conflicts. The histories of both modern and ancient societies are replete with such episodes of violence, and small-scale tribal societies have not been exempt. The decline of Chacoan

Pueblo residents. Much of the emigration probably took place in small groups; in a few cases, whole villages may have traveled together. Warfare and frequent crop failures in the late 1200s must have contributed to the area's depopulation. The trend in the late 1200s of building large villages around springs used for drinking water may also have contributed to rising rates of disease and mortality.

For more than a century, professional archaeologists have failed to find any Pueblo habitation sites dating later than the 1280s in the Mesa Verde area. Yet they have uncovered abundant evidence that down through the centuries, Pueblo people continued to visit shrines and ancestral sites there and perhaps to hunt big game or to trade with the Ute, Paiute, or Navajo people who had moved into the area. Popular writers and filmmakers frequently assert that the

Mesa Verde "Anasazi" simply "disappeared." In fact, archaeological evidence supports Pueblo peoples' traditional knowledge that at least part of their biological and cultural ancestry traces to the Pueblo III communities of the Mesa Verde region.

Widespread warfare and unpredictable rainfall might have made life miserable for the Mesa Verdeans, but it seems unlikely that everyone left for those reasons. The drought of the middle 1100s, after all, was longer and probably more severe than the one of the late 1200s, but in that earlier instance, people hung on until it had passed.

In understanding the depopulation of the Mesa Verde region, "pull" factors—attractions to the south—also need to be considered. Up through the Pueblo II period, the San Juan River drainage was the population center of the Pueblo world. The rise of Chaco made the southern part of this area a hearth of ceremonial, political, and economic influence. That began to change with the waning of Chacoan influence in the early 1100s. Although the Mesa Verde area boomed in the 1200s, so did other parts of the Southwest, such as the Rio Grande, Zuni, and Hopi areas, as well as much of the upper Little Colorado drainage and the Mogollon Rim highlands. By the mid-1200s, many more ancestral Pueblo people lived in these areas than in the Mesa Verde area. Thus, the "center of gravity" of the Pueblo world was definitely shifting southward, leaving the Mesa Verde region isolated on its northern periphery. The depopulation of the late 1200s thus was part of a much larger trend. Migrants from the Mesa Verde region moved to areas that had growing Puebloan populations, where trade networks were flourishing and where different forms of ceremonial practice were associated with more reliable summer rainfall.

Pottery made in the late 1200s and the 1300s in several parts of the Rio Grande area of New Mexico closely resembles Mesa Verde styles, suggesting that Mesa Verde migrants settled there. Other aspects of Pueblo III Mesa Verde culture, however, didn't make the trip. These include the family dwelling unit composed of a small kiva and associated surface rooms that had originated during Pueblo I. Also dropping out were the distinctive public architecture and settlement layouts typical of the late Pueblo III canyon-oriented villages, as well as the characteristic Mesa Verde pottery mugs and kiva jars. Instead of maintaining the patterns they had grown up with, the Mesa Verde migrants adopted new types of kivas, village layouts, and vessel forms. Possibly they had been attracted to religious practices and ways of organizing villages that were already established in their new homelands. Their adoption of new types of architecture and material culture might reflect those more basic changes.

For more than a hundred years, archaeologists and a broad spectrum of the public have been fascinated by the well-preserved sites of the Mesa Verde area. For much longer, the Pueblo peoples of the Southwest have viewed these places as important parts of their cultural heritage. The rich archaeological resources of the Mesa Verde area are of tribal, national, and international importance, and their educational, research, and heritage values are only beginning to be realized.

William D. Lipe is a professor emeritus at Washington State University and a research associate and member of the board at Crow Canyon Archaeological Center in Cortez, Colorado. He has done archaeological research in the Glen Canyon and Cedar Mesa regions of southeastern Utah and the Dolores and McElmo regions of southwestern Colorado. He was senior editor and author of *Colorado Prehistory: The Southern Colorado River Basin*, published in 1999.

Figure 16.1. Members of the Hyde Exploring Expedition's excavation crew in a section of Pueblo Bonito dating to the late 1800s.

A Century of Archaeology in Chaco Canyon

sixteen

Florence C. Lister

In 1896, three white men and several Navajo Indians undertook the first archaeological excavations in Chaco Canyon. Grandly named the Hyde Exploring Expedition, they chose as their site Pueblo Bonito, the largest of nine so-called great houses in the immediate vicinity. Because this immense ruin was situated on public land, no legal restrictions impeded the archaeologists from disturbing it.

Although Pueblo Bonito was mounded over with fallen rubble, windblown dirt, and weeds, the men recognized it as a monumental masonry structure of many rooms several stories in height. They camped at its western end, stored their supplies in some intact ground-level rooms, and commenced work in that part of the site.

Richard Wetherill, a rancher from Mancos, Colorado, who had experience working in cliff dwellings in Colorado and Utah, directed the digging. He was helped by his younger brother Clayton. George Pepper, a twenty-one-year-old novice archaeology student from the East, took notes and cataloged specimens recovered from the earthy deposits that banked some rooms.

Although the excavators did not recognize it at the time, they were exploring the original part of the ruin, which tree-ring experts would date, years later, to the mid-800s CE and archaeologists would place in the Pueblo I phase. Several vacated rooms in this early sector of the dwelling later became burial chambers for some apparently important persons. Wetherill's crew found their bones accompanied by a huge assortment of objects whose quality and quantity remain unmatched elsewhere on the Colorado Plateau.

In 1899, funding for further excavations ceased, and heated protests against the perceived looting of Pueblo Bonito's resources caused the federal government to close down the Hyde Exploring Expedition's activities. This ended the opening chapter of Chaco archaeology on a sour note; nevertheless, much had been accomplished. The workers had removed deposits from 196 of an estimated 650 rooms. Further, they had amassed a staggering volume of specimens, including ten thousand earthenware vessels, five thousand stone implements, fifty thousand turquoise fragments (which once were parts of jewelry and mosaics), many carved wooden staffs, a few foreign copper bells, and pieces of textiles.

Periodically, freighters hauled these artifacts in wagons over miserable dirt tracks to distant railheads from which they were shipped across the continent to the American Museum of Natural History in New York. The museum exhibited some objects for a time but then gradually sequestered them in storage cabinets out of public view, to be forgotten by all but Chaco scholars. Nor did either Wetherill or Pepper ever attempt to interpret the cultural matrix from which the objects came.

After the work at Pueblo Bonito ceased, George Pepper returned to his home base in the East. Westerner Wetherill remained in Chaco Canyon, where he expanded his home compound next to the ruin and concentrated on a ranching and trading enterprise.

Figure 16.2. At the Wetherill trading post in 1899 are, left to right, T. Mitchell Prudden, George H. Pepper, Clayton Wetherill, Mary Wetherill (Clayton's wife), Richard Wetherill Jr., Richard Wetherill, and Marietta Palmer Wetherill.

Meanwhile, in 1906 Congress belatedly passed the Antiquities Act, making it illegal to dig into ruins on federal land without proper authorization. The following year Wetherill voluntarily relinquished his homestead claim, which included Pueblo Bonito, Pueblo del Arroyo, and the western half of Chetro Ketl, and President Theodore Roosevelt set these sites aside as Chaco Canyon National Monument. No visitor or ranger facilities were built at that time. Navajos working for Wetherill carried out some cursory digging in small sites across the canyon.

Three years later Richard Wetherill was killed in Chaco Canyon in an argument with a Navajo (see chapter 9). His remains and those of his widow, who left the canyon after the tragedy, are buried in a dusty plot near the place where Chaco archaeology began.

The Busy Two Decades

Upon the recommendation of Edgar L. Hewett, director of the Museum of New Mexico and the School of American Research, the state of New Mexico gradually acquired title to some of the land

in Chaco Canyon not included in the federal preserve. Just before and after 1920, Hewett planned a limited archaeological investigation of sites on this land. He soon suspended his activities when a larger scientific project was approved for work within the monument.

In 1921 the National Geographic Society, with permits from the National Park Service, underwrote a seven-year campaign to complete the excavation of Pueblo Bonito and to partially expose Pueblo del Arroyo. Under the direction of Neil M. Judd, on loan from the United States National Museum, regional archaeology was transformed from a mere collecting exercise into a discipline with structure and goals. A team of scientists with varied backgrounds focused on artifact analyses and taxonomic standardization, interpretations of the functions of artifacts in daily life, and the ways in which pottery could be used to delineate the evolution of the craft and hence times of manufacture and possible trade networks. In addition, a geologist on the team studied environmental modifications that could have

Figure 16.3. Neil M. Judd.

Figure 16.4. Edgar Lee Hewett, preservationist, teacher, archaeologist, and first director of the School of American Research.

affected the resident populace. Local Navajo and Zuni Pueblo workers screened fill dirt so as not to overlook small items and then used mules and wagons to haul the residue to the nearby wash. Precise measurements of features, detailed record keeping, and photographing were part of every phase of the work.

In short, the National Geographic Society's endeavors in Chaco Canyon added a scientific approach to excavating and employed field methods that were much improved over those of Wetherill's days. In this way, the society provided a firm foundation for future inquiries. Thirty years later, ample data were available to enable Judd to produce a long-awaited report.

Shortly after the Geographic Society project ended, Edgar Hewett returned to Chaco to initiate excavation of the eastern half of Chetro Ketl, the second largest of the Chaco great houses. His primary aim was to use this and other Chaco sites as training grounds for advanced students in the

Department of Anthropology at the University of New Mexico, which he had recently established. In addition to the work at Chetro Ketl, from 1929 through 1935 his students worked at Kin Kletso, a great house west of Pueblo del Arroyo; at a small house next to the talus slope just west of Chetro Ketl; at Leyit Kin, on the south side of the canyon; and at Kin Nahasbas, to the east. Among the students were a number who went on to make names for themselves in regional studies. They included Florence Hawley (Ellis) and Anna Shepard, both ceramic specialists, museum curators Bertha Dutton and Marjorie Lambert, archaeologist Edwin Ferdon, and Paul Reiter, professor of anthropology.

This work in the early 1930s coincided with the successful linking of two sequences of tree-ring dates into a remarkable chronology that extended from the twentieth century back to 700 CE (with tree-ring samples added since then, the sequence now reaches back into the BCE era). Because wood construction elements at Chetro Ketl survived in quantity, the site

Figure 16.5. Gordon Vivian in Chaco Canyon, 1931.

could be precisely dated from the tenth century into the twelfth.

Hewett assigned Gordon Vivian, a promising participant in the fieldwork, the challenging task of excavating the isolated supersanctuary now known as Casa Rinconada, on the south side of the canyon across from Pueblo Bonito and Chetro Ketl. With a sixty-four-foot diameter, it proved to be the largest great kiva in the canyon and one of the finest examples of ancestral Pueblo construction.

By the 1930s, government administrators recognized that once fragile edifices of stone set in unreinforced mud were exposed to the elements, they quickly deteriorated, so preserving America's antiquities required constant maintenance. Therefore, in 1933, Gordon Vivian was hired to train a crew of Navajo men to make unobtrusive repairs to ruins, first in Chaco Canyon and later throughout the Southwest. In this way, a subcraft

of stabilization came into being that continues actively to the present.

In the summer of 1936, the Department of Anthropology at the University of New Mexico began an archaeological field school in Chaco Canyon for undergraduates as well as advanced students. At first the participants were quartered in tents in the old Wetherill compound, but within two years a permanent facility was built along the south canyon cliffs next to Casa Rinconada. Over the course of six summers, hundreds of young men and women from across the country came to Chaco Canyon, not only to learn proper digging techniques but also to become familiar with the gamut of past and present regional life under the tutelage of a college faculty. Removed from the outside world's distractions, with a Native American presence at hand and some of North America's most impressive prehistoric remains at every turn, it was a superb laboratory. The work of these students and staff members added a new dimension to the ancient drama by revealing a series of small houses that were coeval with but totally distinctive from the great houses lined up on the north side of the canyon. The staff assumed that Casa Rinconada had been placed in the midst of the small houses as a means of integrating the villagers into a larger society across the canyon. A gift to science that came out of the field schools was the basic field training received by many later participants in American archaeology.

The Interlude

The field school closed in 1942 with the disruptions of the Second World War. Because research is not part of the mandate of the National Park Service, for a number of years federal archaeologists undertook no further excavation except when physical developments in the monument were expected to affect known antiquities or when a structure appeared to be in a precarious condition.

A case in point was the great house Kin Kletso, in mid-canyon, when its high, jagged walls threatened to collapse. In the 1950s, Vivian and Park Service archaeologist Thomas Matthews completely cleared and stabilized this fifty-room structure, thus both preserving it and enhancing the monument's interpretive program. Kin Kletso has a different plan

Figure 16.6. Gwinn Vivian with Florence Lister.

and masonry style from those of other great houses. Scholars attribute the differences to people or ideas that they believe drifted into Chaco from the northern San Juan region late in the twelfth century.

The remains of dried plants, such as corncobs and squash rinds, that had been excavated during the first work in Pueblo Bonito made it apparent that Chaco Canyon's inhabitants had sustained themselves in part by rudimentary farming. To discover how that might have been accomplished in Chaco's inhospitable environment, Gwinn Vivian, Gordon's son, began a long-term study. He sought possible ways these Puebloans might have captured and used natural precipitation to their advantage over a period of perhaps three centuries (see chapter 2).

The Climax

John Corbett was a veteran of the 1936 university field school in Chaco Canyon; thirty years later he was chief archaeologist of the National Park Service. In light of a surge of investigations taking place in the 1960s on the Colorado Plateau and the refined analytical and methodological techniques that had evolved by then, he believed that further Chaco research was warranted. Corbett's persistent lobbying of officialdom culminated in the establishment of the Chaco Center in 1971. It was to be jointly sponsored for ten years by the National Park Service and the University of New Mexico. Robert H. Lister, a professor of anthropology at the University of Colorado, a longtime National Park Service collaborator, and a onetime chief archaeologist for the National Park Service, headed this organization. Its aim was to bring a multidisciplinary approach to bear on the understanding of the past. After directing the research program for five years, Lister passed the assignment to W. James Judge, who stayed with the project until its termination.

As an initial step, the Chaco Center made an exhaustive survey of forty-three square miles of the canyon and its surroundings to determine the extent of the cultural resources present. Such a study had never before been attempted. Alden C. Hayes, another veteran Park Service archaeologist, directed the survey, his team walking and rewalking the territory to tabulate twenty-two hundred archaeological features. These ranged from scatters of stone flakes to rock art and architectural constructions. The team concluded that the seeming wasteland they surveyed had been utilized or inhabited by many ancient peoples. Hayes estimated the peak population of Chaco Canyon at approximately six thousand; later researchers considered that figure too high.

Excavators opened a series of sites representing all the cultural stages the surveyors had identified. These sites included Atlatl Cave, used by Archaic hunter-gatherers, pithouses occupied by the first sedentary farmers, and the great house Pueblo Alto. During this fertile period of field research, a variety of other sites were studied: a network of roads; rock dams and gridded gardens; a unique solstice-marker petroglyph (popularly called the "sun dagger") atop prominent Fajada Butte; and a pictograph panel thought to record the Crab Nebula supernova that was visible in the heavens in 1054. The solstice-marker discovery, especially, received a flood of publicity that brought waves of tourists to the monument.

Figure 16.7. Robert Lister in Atlatl Cave, Chaco Canyon.

Figure 16.8. W. James Judge.

Although archaeologists had long known of a few Chaco-style structures outside the canyon, the revitalized concern with things Chacoan in the 1970s and 1980s made scientists aware of the Chaco world's extent over most of the San Juan Basin and beyond. Researchers found that the outlying great houses, in addition to having been built in the architectural modes of Chaco at its eleventh-century zenith, were situated in or next to indigenous communities. Also,

they were closely associated with enigmatic road segments. In 1980 these new discoveries prompted the Park Service to incorporate some of the outlying great houses into an enlarged entity that was named Chaco Culture National Historical Park.

The Chaco Center's work confirmed the existence of a society far more complex than had previously been recognized, but also one that begged for broad anthropological considerations of its social, political, and economic structure. One overarching question—as yet unanswered—concerns the spark that ignited the florescence in Chaco Canyon in the mid-1000s, setting its residents so apart from neighboring ancestral Pueblos. Another is why the culture fizzled out early in the next century. Without documentation from the Chacoans themselves, answers will never be to everyone's satisfaction. Still, what started out a century ago as a treasure hunt now has scientific substance to greatly enhance the contributions afforded by the study of Chacoan prehistory.

Florence Lister is an anthropologist, historian, and prolific writer. Her books include *Pot Luck: Adventures in Archaeology*; *In the Shadow of the Rocks: Archaeology of the Chimney Rock District in Southern Colorado*; and, with her late husband, Robert Lister, *Chaco Canyon: Archaeology and Archaeologists*.

Key Debates in Chacoan Archaeology

Barbara J. Mills

Archaeology at Chaco Canyon has undergone a transformation since the early 1980s. Lamentably, this is not because of new excavations. Happily, it is because a dynamic group of archaeologists, tied together by their love of Chacoan archaeology, have incorporated new methods and theories into their work. Some of these researchers have worked at Chaco for a long time. Others are recent additions to the Chaco archaeological community. All share an interest in fathoming what happened in the past in Chaco Canyon and the surrounding region by testing previous interpretations with new theories. Not all archaeologists interpret what happened at Chaco in the same way, however—particularly what happened during the crucial Bonito phase (920–1120 CE). By briefly describing a few of the key debates, I want to offer readers an intellectual compass for mapping the landscape of Chacoan archaeology in the early twenty-first century.

How Big Was Chaco?

Today, visitors to Chaco Canyon travel along seemingly endless dirt roads into the heart of the San Juan Basin. When Chaco was at its peak population during the eleventh and early twelfth centuries, this stark landscape was dotted with communities that replicated key architectural attributes found in the canyon. These key features included great houses surrounded by clusters of small houses, circular great kivas, and road segments. Just how big the greater Chacoan population was and how large an area was included in the region of Chacoan influence are two of the key debates.

Some scholars argue for a vast regional system that extended well beyond the boundaries of the San Juan Basin. Stephen Lekson has called this the "Anasazi regional system" to underscore the extensive territory that shared Chacoan architecture and, presumably, many other aspects of Chacoan society, such as its ritual and domestic organization. His region covers a huge part of the Colorado Plateau. Other scholars, such as Gwinn Vivian, draw a smaller region—largely coeval with the physiographic zone of the San Juan Basin. Most archaeologists agree, however, that outlying communities in southeastern Utah, southwestern Colorado, eastern Arizona, and west-central New Mexico share too many Chacoan architectural characteristics to be excluded from discussions of Chacoan archaeology.

The size of the Chacoan region is important for many interpretations about Chacoan society and the influence Chaco held over outlying communities. It is especially crucial for understanding who might have traveled to and from "downtown" Chaco, how many people might have considered themselves part of the greater Chacoan society, and what kind of leadership might have been present to account for the seemingly uniform construction of Chacoan great houses and great kivas across such a vast part of the Southwest.

Jeffrey Dean and his coauthors proposed that the population of the greater Chaco region was fifty-five thousand persons at around 1000 CE. This contrasts with estimates for the population of Chaco Canyon itself of two thousand to six thousand persons. The lower end of this estimate was

Figure 17.1. Chaco Project archaeologists at Pueblo Alto. Front row, left to right: Peter McKenna, Tom Windes, Marcia Truell, and Jim Judge, director of the Chaco Center. Second row: John Schelberg, Nancy Akins, LouAnn Jacobson, Cory Breternitz, Bob Powers, Wolky Toll, and Marcia Donaldson. Third row: Bill Greenlee, Sandra Diepen. Fourth row: Steve Lekson, Bill Gillespie, Chip Wills, B. Ratti, S. Roll. J. Martinez, M. Britt, E. Garcia, Daniel Lopez, Gerald Harrison, A. Hasuse.

was developed by Thomas Windes, who noticed that great houses each contained only a small number of residential suites—groups of interconnected rooms that were each occupied by a single residential group or household. By counting residential suites, he estimated that Pueblo Bonito housed a maximum of only eighteen households and a total population of about one hundred people. His estimate has been confirmed by subsequent research. Most archaeologists working in the area now agree that a relatively small group of people resided in the canyon and that an even smaller group resided in its great houses.

How did such a small number of people influence residents of communities across such a vast region? This question sits at the heart of debates about Chacoan society and leads us to consider how leadership was instituted and maintained.

What Was the Nature of Chacoan Leadership?

All societies have leaders, and Chaco was no exception. Nonetheless, leadership at Chaco is one of the most widely debated topics among current investigators. Their debates center on three key variables: whether Chacoan society was organized hierarchically

Figure 17.2. The fine masonry styles apparent in Chaco Canyon great houses are reflected in outlying great houses.

or along more egalitarian lines; whether leadership was centralized or dispersed among a number of different individuals and communities; and what constituted the varied sources of leaders' power. Attention to these variables marks an important shift in archaeological thinking about Chaco. Instead of asking whether Chaco was a complex society, scholars are asking, How was Chaco complex?

Until recently, archaeologists assumed that hierarchical organization could not be a part of Southwestern Puebloan society, past or present. Historic and contemporary descriptions of Pueblo societies in the Southwest almost uniformly emphasize the collective over the individual. Recently, however, many cultural anthropologists and archaeologists have begun to recognize that Pueblo societies are less egalitarian than once thought. Archaeologists have also recognized that ancestral Pueblo societies might have been structured very differently from historic and contemporary ones. This observation is especially true of researchers working at Chaco and has resulted in many new interpretations of Chacoan leadership.

Archaeological data from Chaco Canyon indicate a degree of social differentiation much greater than

that documented for historic Pueblo societies (see chapter 13). Residents of the great houses appear to have had better access to resources than others and as a result enjoyed better health. They accumulated more turquoise and other rare artifacts that suggest fundamental social differences. At Pueblo Bonito, related individuals were buried in clusters that suggest long-standing family lineages. People in these clusters, including children, had greater numbers of rare artifacts buried with them than did people buried elsewhere in the site. Nancy Akins, biological archaeologist for the National Park Service's Chaco Project, believes these children to have been members of important lineages with inherited, rather than achieved, social status. Although there are still some dissenting voices, many archaeologists would agree with Jill Neitzel's recent assessment that these data support the idea that some kind of social hierarchy existed at Chaco Canyon.

A key point of controversy remains—namely, whether hierarchical leadership must go hand in hand with centralized power. In the past, archaeologists assumed that when the few ruled the many, leadership had to be centralized in a few key positions within each society. This assumption has been widely challenged by archaeologists working throughout the world who argue that leadership may be dispersed across a number of different positions, each of which has a different set of rules for determining who will fill that role.

Some archaeologists hold to the interpretation that leadership at Chaco was both socially and spatially centralized. Others suggest that there were many leaders, dispersed among different leadership roles and great houses throughout the wider region. David Wilcox, from the Museum of Northern Arizona, is one who agrees with the former

Figure 17.3. Three containers full of turquoise beads excavated from Pueblo Bonito by the Hyde Exploring Expedition, 1896.

interpretation. He sees a highly centralized social and political system in which the residents of Chaco Canyon held a great degree of control over the region. He has even argued that the Chacoan great houses might have housed a standing army.

Other archaeologists, like myself, accept that a hierarchical organization existed at Chaco but believe it was dispersed among a number of different leadership positions. Each position would have had its own principles of recruitment and its own roles within Chacoan society, drawing upon ritual, economic, political, and kinship networks. In addition, these positions were spatially dispersed throughout the Chaco region. Evidence to support the last interpretation lies in the tremendous amount of architectural and artifactual variation we see in the Chaco region. For example, John Kantner, Daniel Meyer, and Ruth Van Dyke each have analyzed community layouts and construction techniques throughout the San Juan Basin. Independently, they found that sufficient differences exist among Chacoan outlier communities to argue for a lack of control by Chaco Canyon residents.

The final question currently being debated about Chacoan leadership is how those leaders were

able to acquire and maintain their power. Was it economic, ritual, or some combination of the two? If power was ritual, was it based in a single form of ceremonial organization such as a rain priesthood or were there multiple, cross-cutting ceremonial societies? And were leaders coercive or cooperative? Lynne Sebastian has argued that leaders initially secured their positions through the production and exchange of surplus food. She found that periods of exceptionally good agricultural productivity prevailed at the time Chacoan leadership first developed in the tenth century. Later on, however, it appears that leadership shifted to include a greater emphasis on ritual power.

The emphasis on ritual leadership seems to be gaining support among archaeologists writing about Chaco. They cite the large number of votive offerings found at Pueblo Bonito, including cylinder jars and turquoise, as well as the inordinate amount of trash discarded at great houses relative to their small populations. Further evidence of intense ceremonial activity—a cache of painted wooden ritual artifacts that Gwinn Vivian and his colleagues convincingly compared to historic and contemporary altarpieces—was uncovered at the Chacoan great house Chetro Ketl. These various lines of evidence led H. Wolcott Toll, W. James Judge, Stephen Lekson, and other archaeologists who were part of the National Park Service's Chaco Center in the 1970s and 1980s to propose a model of Chaco as a pilgrimage site, with Chacoan residents as hosts to periodic visitors from around the San Juan Basin.

The pilgrimage fair model is still popular with many archaeologists who see Chaco as a center of ritual activity in the San Juan Basin. Indeed, as David Doyel points out, many of the outlying Chacoan communities closest to Chaco Canyon—which he calls the "Chaco halo"—do not have associated great kivas and probably participated in canyon ritual activities. And as John Kantner suggests (see chapter 10), many of the Chacoan roads are only short segments that appear to have been used as ritual pathways rather than as a basinwide, interconnecting road system.

Figure 17.4. Three outstanding examples of Pueblo Bonito's cylinder jars. Most of the total of 122 jars, however, which excavators found in three rooms, were undecorated.

The major argument against ritual as the source of leaders' power has been voiced by W. H. Wills. He observes that it is nonritual architecture that took the greatest labor to construct and that ritual artifacts are rare at all sites except Pueblo Bonito. He also points out that the trash mounds might contain considerably more construction fill than was originally thought, which would bias interpretations of the actual amount of trash discarded in these places. He suggests that leaders of individual lineages organized the construction of great houses on an annual basis and that leaders' ability to mobilize enough labor to procure materials and construct the massive roomblocks was the source of their power.

Debates about how leaders achieved their power also center on whether that power was coercive or cooperative. Several archaeologists—Ruth Van Dyke and John Kantner, for example—adhere to the idea that leaders must use force, or the threat of force, in order to have followers. Their approach contrasts

with that of Ben Nelson and Gwinn Vivian, who see leaders as the heads of cooperative groups. If leaders were the heads of related families or lineages, then this would lend more credence to the idea of communal leadership, because people are more likely to cooperate with those with whom they have connections by birth. Lineages were clearly important at Chaco, as the burial clusters from Pueblo Bonito demonstrate. However, it is my belief that all societies display wide variation in the way people take charge and the way they use their power. Chacoan leaders were probably no exception.

Chacoan Exchange

One of the things archaeologists agree about is that a wide variety of materials was transported into Chaco Canyon (see chapter 5). It included wood, stone, pottery, turquoise, shell, parrots, feathers, and probably many kinds of foods. Archaeologists have become increasingly skilled at figuring out where things come from, something also known as "provenance." What they do not agree about is how these items got to Chaco and why.

If the items brought to Chaco were all rare ones, then it could be argued that some of the residents of Chaco used them to build personal relationships with people inside and outside of the Chacoan area—that is, they took part in an economy based on prestige. But the bulk of the items that came into Chaco were not the kinds of materials anyone would think of as rare: architectural wood, pottery, chert. Moreover, it appears that large portions of the Chaco Canyon community had access to all these materials, even if those living in the great houses had more than others.

The carrying of an enormous amount of architectural wood into Chaco Canyon, estimated to represent more than two hundred thousand trees, was an amazing feat for a society without wheeled vehicles, boat transportation, or pack animals. Chemical and chronological analyses of the wood performed by Nathan English, Julio Betancourt, Jeffrey Dean, and Jay Quade of the University of Arizona indicate that starting in the late tenth century, much of the wood found at Chaco came from a limited number of sources, especially the Chuska Mountains more than forty-three miles to the west. Tom Windes has suggested that the amount of wood procured indicates a great degree of planning and specialized

silvaculture but that small work parties could have accomplished the wood felling, beam preparation, and transport. Similarly, Melissa Hagstrum has noted that the flexibility of household pottery production can account for the large amounts of pottery made outside of Chaco. For example, a relatively small number of households could expand their output to make pottery for many other households.

The biggest debate about the importation of large amounts of nonlocal materials concerns whether these items were brought to Chaco by residents of outlying communities or whether Chacoan residents periodically left the canyon to procure such items themselves. On one hand, residents of Chaco might have organized wood procurement parties to go to the Chuskas. Household members might also have made pottery, which is so dependent on wood for firing, in the mountains. On the other hand, residents of the Chuskas might have made regular pilgrimages to Chaco, bringing with them wood, pottery, stone (especially chert), and perhaps food. As with many other debates, I think that what happened in the past may have been a little bit of both.

Conflict and Violence

The topics of warfare and cannibalism are receiving increasingly widespread attention in both the professional and the popular literature. Judging from comparative research around the globe, it is extremely unlikely that ancestral Pueblo people experienced conflict-free lives. Today, the nature of their conflicts is one of the most hotly debated topics among Southwesternists, including those working on Chacoan archaeology.

Despite the fact that small agricultural societies worldwide are replete with conflict, and despite some recent compelling evidence for the consumption of human flesh elsewhere in the Southwest, evidence for violence at Chaco is remarkably scarce. Indeed, Stephen LeBlanc, of Harvard's Peabody Museum, has pointed out that Chaco stands out from the rest of the Southwest in showing very little evidence for violence. This was especially

Figure 17.5. A ceiling in Pueblo Bonito. More than two hundred thousand tree trunks are estimated to have been carried to Chaco Canyon from distant areas such as the Chuska Mountains for great-house construction.

Figure 17.6. Participants in a seminar on Chaco digital archives held at the School of American Research in July 2003. Left to right: Dabney Ford, Wendy Bustard, Gwinn Vivian, Jim Judge, Joan Mathien.

the case at the time of Chaco's peak occupation, from 900 to 1150, during what Stephen Lekson refers to as the Pax Chaco. Similarly, Wendy Bustard of the National Park Service has reviewed putative evidence for violence in the northern Southwest and found that most cases date later than 1150 and therefore are post-Chacoan, or else they took place in the Mesa Verde area and were not Chacoan at all.

Why Did People Leave?

Most people who come to Chaco ask, Why did the Chacoans leave after investing so much labor in the construction of great houses, great kivas, and roads? One thing to keep in mind when thinking about ancestral Pueblo society is that migration was a way of life. The Southwestern landscape is full of stopping-off places—villages where people lived for perhaps only a generation or two. Chaco Canyon villages were long-lived compared to many of these. After living at Chaco, its residents moved on to found other villages or join other communities with which they had long-standing ties. Post-Chacoan villages can be found on the Chuska slopes, along the San Juan River and its tributaries, and in the Zuni area. These, too, were stopping-off points for ancestral Pueblo people who eventually moved to the historic and modern pueblos in New Mexico and Arizona.

Why they chose to leave when they did, however, is an important question. Although environmental explanations have fallen out of favor in archaeology, a large body of evidence suggests that the timing of the migration out of Chaco Canyon was related to a deterioration of the environment. A prolonged drought that affected the entire San Juan Basin after 1130 appears to have caused major disruption in Chacoan society.

Reconstructing specific migration pathways out of Chaco has been a major research effort by contemporary archaeologists and bioarchaeologists. Stephen Lekson has proposed that Chacoans first migrated to Aztec on the Animas River and then followed a direct line, or meridian, south to the Casas Grandes village of Paquimé in northern Chihuahua. Although many scholars agree with Lekson about the first migration, his argument for the second migration, which would have taken Chacoans hundreds of miles to the south, is more hotly debated. In contrast to this interpretation, bioarchaeologists point out that Chacoans show genetic ties to Pueblo groups in the Rio Grande, Acoma, Zuni, and Hopi areas. And members of these Pueblo groups, representing several different languages, have place-names for Chaco. Thus, it seems clear that although Chaco Canyon was depopulated, its residents did not disappear—they moved on, at least some of

Figure 17.7. Santo Domingo Pueblo, 1880. Some present-day Pueblo groups in the Rio Grande, Acoma, Zuni, and Hopi areas are believed to have ancestral links to Chaco Canyon.

them joining other Puebloan people across the Colorado Plateau. Moreover, Chaco culture did not "collapse," as has so often been stated in the past— it was transformed through a series of events that archaeologists are just beginning to identify.

New Debates

Archaeologists continually apply new methods and theories to interpret the past, and Southwesternists are no exception. Chaco Canyon offers an important context in which researchers can use their new approaches, which are increasingly focused in two major directions. The first is the application of scientific instrumentation in order to understand where things came from, how they were made, and what they might have been used for. We will see major new findings as different forms of scientific instrumentation are applied to Chacoan archaeology. As a result, we will also see some new debates emerge and some old ones resolved.

The other direction archaeologists are taking is toward what many refer to as social archaeology, or the understanding of past social dynamics. This includes interpretations about how identity was expressed, how social interaction was structured,

and how daily life was practiced and reproduced over time. We may never know what people really thought in the past, but we can apply new social theories to understand more fully how people lived. Because these theories are difficult to apply, the results will be debated. But they will also add considerable depth to our understanding of past societies, including the one that flourished for so short a time at Chaco Canyon.

Barbara J. Mills is a professor of anthropology at the University of Arizona. She has conducted extensive field and laboratory research on Chacoan sites, including archaeological survey in Chaco Culture National Historical Park. Her overview of Chacoan archaeology, "Recent Research on Chaco: Changing Views on Economy, Ritual, and Society," appeared in the March 2002 issue of the *Journal of Archaeological Research*.

Suggested Reading

American Antiquity
2001   Special section on the organization of production in Chaco Canyon. *American Antiquity* 66:1. Washington, D.C.: Society for American Archaeology.

Brugge, David M.
1980   *A History of the Chaco Navajos.* Reports of the Chaco Center, no. 4. Albuquerque, N.M.: National Park Service, Division of Chaco Research.

Cordell, Linda S., W. James Judge, and June-el Piper, eds.
2001   *Chaco Society and Polity: Papers from the 1999 Conference.* Special Publication 4. Albuquerque: New Mexico Archaeological Council.

Doyel, David E., ed.
1992   *Anasazi Regional Organization and the Chaco System.* Anthropological Papers no. 5. Albuquerque: Maxwell Museum of Anthropology, University of New Mexico.

Hayes, Alden C., David M. Brugge, and W. James Judge
1981   *Archaeological Surveys of Chaco Canyon, New Mexico.* Publications in Archaeology 18A: Chaco Canyon Studies. Washington, D.C.: National Park Service.

Kantner, John, and Nancy M. Mahoney, eds.
2000   *Great House Communities across the Chacoan Landscape.* Tucson: University of Arizona Press.

Kincaid, Chris, ed.
1983   *Chaco Roads Project, Phase 1: A Reappraisal of Prehistoric Roads in the San Juan Basin 1983.* Albuquerque: Bureau of Land Management.

Lekson, Stephen H.
1999   *The Chaco Meridian: Centers of Political Power in the Ancient Southwest.* Walnut Creek, Calif.: Altamira Press.

Lister, Robert H., and Florence C. Lister
1981   *Chaco Canyon: Archaeology and Archaeologists.* Albuquerque: University of New Mexico Press.

Malville, J. McKim
1989   *Prehistoric Astronomy in the Southwest.* Boulder, Colo.: Johnson Books.

Mills, Barbara J.
2001   "Recent Research on Chaco: Changing Views on Economy, Ritual, and Society." *Journal of Archaeological Research* 10(1):65–117.

Neitzel, Jill, ed.
2001   *Pueblo Bonito: Center of the Chacoan World.* Washington, D.C.: Smithsonian Institution Press.

Sebastian, Lynne
1992   *The Chaco Anasazi: Sociopolitical Evolution in the Prehistoric Southwest.* Cambridge: Cambridge University Press.

Sofaer, Anna, dir.
1999   *The Mystery of Chaco Canyon.* Oley, Pa.: Bullfrog Films.

Sofaer, Anna, Michael P. Marshall, and Rolf M. Sinclair
1989   *"The Great North Road: A Cosmographic Expression of the Chaco Culture of New Mexico."* In *World Archaeoastronomy*, edited by Anthony F. Aveni, pp. 365–76. Cambridge: Cambridge University Press.

Strutin, Michal, with photography by George H. H. Huey
1994   *Chaco: A Cultural Legacy.* Tucson: Southwest Parks and Monuments Association.

Vivian, Gordon, and Tom W. Matthews
1965   *Kin Kletso: A Pueblo III Community in Chaco Canyon, New Mexico.* Southwestern Monuments Association Technical Series, vol. 6, no. 1. Globe, AZ.

Vivian, R. Gwinn
1990   *The Chacoan Prehistory of the San Juan Basin.* New York: Academic Press.

Vivian, R. Gwinn and Bruce Hilpert
2002   *The Chaco Handbook: An Encyclopedia Guide.* Salt Lake City: University of Utah Press.

Picture Credits

color section, after page 30

The massive Pueblo Bonito with the canyon cliffs rising behind. Photograph by David Grant Noble

Excavators at work at Pueblo Alto, late 1970s. Courtesy National Park Service, Chaco Culture National Historical Park, Museum Collection.

Pueblo Pintado great house. Photograph by William Stone.

Chetro Ketl's tower kiva. Photograph by David Grant Noble.

Artists' reconstruction of Kin Hocho'i outlying great house. Drawing by Robert and Karen Turner

Peñasco Blanco great house, west end of Chaco Canyon. Photograph by William Stone.

A fourteen-foot-long necklace of shell and stone beads, along with three pieces of turquoise, all from a wall niche in Chetro Ketl's great kiva. Collections of the Museum of New Mexico. Photograph by Deborah Flynn.

Chaco corrugated jar (1075–1225) excavated from Kin Kletso. Courtesy Chaco Culture National Historical Park. Photograph by George H. H. Huey.

Craft arts from Pueblo Bonito excavated by the Hyde Exploring Expedition of 1896–1899 and now in the American Museum of Natural History. Left: reconstructed turquoise-encrusted cylinder; center: deer bone spatula or scraper inlaid with jet and turquoise; right: McElmo Black-on-white pitcher. Photograph by Deborah Flynn.

A McElmo Black-on-white pottery canteen from Chetro Ketl. Collections of the Museum of Indian Arts and Culture/Laboratory of Anthropology, Museum of New Mexico. Photograph by Deborah Flynn.

color section, after page 94

Pictograph, ancestral Pueblo handprints on Chacra Mesa. Courtesy National Park Service, Chaco Culture National Historical Park.

Guadalupe Pueblo. In the distance are the Rio Puerco and Cabezon Peak. Photograph by William Stone.

Chaco Wash in a summer flood. Photograph by George H. H. Huey.

Petroglyph panel in Chaco Canyon showing humpbacked flute players and other figures. Photograph by David Grant Noble.

Kivas in morning fog at Pueblo Bonito. This great house includes thirty-three kivas. Photograph by George H. H. Huey.

Pueblo del Arroyo in winter. Photograph by George H. H. Huey.

View of the central-western portion of Chaco Canyon, with Pueblo Bonito at bottom center and Pueblo del Arroyo immediately above it along Chaco Wash. Photograph by Adriel Heisey.

Chimney Rock great house in foreground with the spires of Chimney Rock behind. Photograph by Adriel Heisey.

front matter

ii, Charles A. Lindbergh, courtesy, Museum of New Mexico, neg. no. 130232; x, xii, Maps by Molly O'Halloran; xiii, Matts Myhrman; xv, David Grant Noble.

chapter one

xviii, Kent Bowser; 2, Paul Logsdon; 3, David Grant Noble; 4, Courtesy Museum of New Mexico; 5, Diagram by Katrina Lasko, adapted from Stephen H. Lekson, *Great Pueblo Architecture of Chaco Canyon* (University of New Mexico Press, 1986); 6, David Grant Noble.

chapter two

8, David Grant Noble; 9, Diagram by Katrina Lasko, adapted from figure 4 in William C. Allen, "Present and Past Climate," in *Settlement and Subsistence along the Lower Chaco River*, edited by Charles A. Reher (University of New Mexico Press, 1977); 10, 13, R. Gwinn Vivian; 11, Courtesy Museum of New Mexico; 12, Drawing by Katrina Lasko after Amy Elizabeth Gray in Stephen Plog, *Ancient Peoples of the American Southwest*. New York: Thames and Hudson, fig. 91.

chapter three

14, H. Wolcott Toll; 17, Drawing by Katrina Lasko, adapted from figure 2.9 in Joel M. Brisbin, Allen E. Kane, and James N. Morris, "Excavations at McPhee Pueblo (Site 5MT4475), a Pueblo I and Early Pueblo II Multi-component Village," in *Dolores Archaeological Program: Anasazi Communities at Dolores; McPhee Village*, compiled by A. E. Kane and C. K. Robinson (US Department of the Interior, Bureau of Reclamation, Engineering and Research Center, Denver, Colorado, 1988); 18 (top) courtesy Bureau of Land Management; (bottom) David Grant Noble; 19, Courtesy Thomas Windes, National Park Service; 20, Paul Logsdon.

chapter four

22, George A. Grant. Courtesy Western Archaeological and Conservation Center, Museum Collection Repository Archives Program; 24, Drawing by Patricia McCreery; 25, David Grant Noble; 27, George A. Grant, 1929. Courtesy Western Archaeological and Conservation Center, Museum Collection Repository Archives Program; 28, David Grant Noble; 30, Courtesy National Park Service, Chaco Culture National Historical Park, Museum Collection; 31, Paul Logsdon.

chapter five
32, Mary Peck. Courtesy Museum of Indian Arts and Culture/Laboratory of Anthropology, Museum of New Mexico, www.miaclab.org. Catalog number 08552/11. Museum purchase from C. G. Wallace, Zuni, 1935; **34**, David Grant Noble; **35**, Deborah Flynn. Credit data: left to right, collections of the National Park Service; collections of the Maxwell Museum of Anthropology, University of New Mexico; collections of the American Museum of Natural History; **36**, graph by H. Wolcott Toll; **37**, Courtesy Museum of New Mexico, neg. no. 6137; **39**, Courtesy Museum of Indian Arts and Culture/Laboratory of Anthropology Archives, Museum of New Mexico.

chapter six
42, David Grant Noble; **43**, Collections of the American Museum of Natural History; **44**, R. Gwinn Vivian; **45**, David Grant Noble; **47** (top) David Grant Noble; (bottom) Paul Logsdon.

chapter seven
48, William Stone; **50**, **51**, David Grant Noble; **52**, Courtesy Museum of New Mexico, neg. no. 66982.

chapter eight
54, **60**, David Grant Noble; **56**, Adriel Heisey; **57**, **58**, Courtesy National Park Service, Chaco Culture National Historical Park, Museum Collection; **59**, Lewis Murphy, Courtesy National Park Service, Chaco Culture National Historical Park, Museum Collection; **59**, Florence Hawley. Courtesy National Park Service, Chaco Culture National Park, Museum Collection.

chapter nine
62, Map by Molly O'Halloran; **63** (top) David Grant Noble; (bottom) Courtesy National Park Service; **65**, George Pepper. Courtesy New Mexico State Records Center and Archives, McNitt Collection, neg no. 5873; **67**, David Grant Noble; **68**, Courtesy National Park Service, Chaco Culture National Historical Park, Museum Collection; **69**, Photographer unknown. Courtesy Navajo Tribal Museum.

chapter ten
70, David Grant Noble; **72**, Map by Molly O'Halloran with the assistance of John Kantner; **74**, Adapted from *Great House Communities Across the Chacoan Landscape*, edited by John Kantner and Nancy M. Mahoney. © 2000 The Arizona Board of Regents. Reprinted by permission of the University of Arizona Press. **75**, Robert Buettner. Courtesy R. Gwinn Vivian; **77**, David Grant Noble.

chapter eleven
78, **81**, **82**, Ruth Van Dyke; **83**, Paul Logsdon, 1984; **84**, Adriel Heisey; **85**, Milo McCloud. Courtesy National Park Service, Chaco Culture National Historical Park, Museum Collection.

chapter twelve
86, Karl Kernberger. Courtesy Carolyn Kernberger; **88**, J. McKim Malville; **89**, **90** (top) David Grant Noble; (bottom) J. McKim Malville; **92**, J. McKim Malville; **91**, G. B. Cornucopia.

chapter thirteen
94, David Grant Noble; **96**, Courtesy John R. Stein, Dabney Ford, and Richard Friedman; **97**, David Grant Noble; **98**, Collections of the American Museum of Natural History. Photograph by Deborah Flynn; **99**, H. Wolcott Toll.

chapter fourteen
100, Kent Bowser; **102**, Robert Buettner. Courtesy R. Gwinn Vivian; **103**, R. Hill. Courtesy Malta Tourist Office; **104**, Map by Molly O'Halloran; **105**, Collections of the American Museum of Natural History; **106**, Robert A. Ellison, Jr.

chapter fifteen
108,**111**,**114**, David Grant Noble; **109**, Drawing by Patricia McCreery; **110**, Paul Logsdon; **112**, Drawing by Jerry Livingston, courtesy National Park Service.

chapter sixteen
116, Courtesy American Museum of Natural History; **118**, Courtesy National Park Service, Chaco Culture National Historical Park, Museum Collection; **119**, Courtesy National Park Service, Chaco Culture National Historical Park, Museum Collection; **119**, Courtesy Museum of New Mexico, neg. no. 7374; **120**, **121**, Courtesy R. Gwinn Vivian; **122**, (top) Courtesy Florence Lister; (bottom) Courtesy National Park Service, Chaco Culture National Historical Park, Museum Collection.

chapter seventeen
124, Courtesy National Park Service, Chaco Culture National Historical Park, Museum Collection; **125**, David Grant Noble; **126**, Courtesy American Museum of Natural History; **127**, Deborah Flynn. Collections of the American Museum of Natural History; **128**, Courtesy Museum of Indian Arts and Culture and Laboratory of Anthropology Archives, Museum of New Mexico; **129**, School of American Research Collections, photograph by Katrina Lasko; **130**, George C. Bennett. Courtesy Museum of New Mexico, neg. no. 4357.

Index

Note: page numbers printed in *italics* refer to figures.

Doyel, David, 126
droughts: and collapse of Chaco system, 6, 13, 129; in contemporary Southwest, 53; and depopulation of Mesa Verde region, 112, 114, 115. *See also* climate
Durand, Kathy Roler, 76
Dutton, Bertha, 119

East Community, 21
Easter Island, and ritual centers, 102East Road, 83
economics, and Chaco Canyon as ritual center, 105. *See also* agriculture; importation; labor; trade
Eddy, Frank, 111
egalitarianism, and sociopolitical organization in Chaco Canyon, 95, 101, 106
El Malpais, 80
elites, and great houses of Chaco Canyon, 27, 31
English, Nathan, 128
environment, of Chaco Canyon: and agriculture, 7, 9-11; and aridity of San Juan Basin, 6; and emergence of cultural complexity, 1; and Hopi oral tradition, 42; and migration out of Chaco Canyon, 129; and natural resources for artifacts, 33-34. *See also* climate; landscape
Escalante Ruin (Colorado), 111
Escalon site, 81, *82*
Escavada Wash, 1, 2, *32*
exchange. *See* importation; trade
exotic materials, and artifacts, 37-39. *See also* copper bells; macaws; turquoise

Fajada Butte, *2, 8, 50*: and astronomical alignments, 16, 83-84, 88, 91; and petroglyphs, 83-84, 87, *88*; and Navajo in Chaco region, 58
Fajada Wash, 16
Ferdon, Edwin, 119
Fewkes, Jesse Walter, 81
Finn, Will, 67
Fowler, Andrew, 29, 84
food shortages, social adaptation to in Chaco Canyon, 11-13. *See also* agriculture; droughts
Ford, Dabney, *129*
Freeman, Katy, 29
Friedman, Richard, 29
Fritz, John, 28

gambling, and Navajo oral tradition, 56
Garcia, E., *124*
geochemical analyses, of artifacts, 77
geographic information systems (GIS), 77
geography. *See* landscape

geology, and sources of clays and stone for artifacts, 33
Gillespie, William, 9, *124*
Great Depression, and Navajo, 68
great houses, of Chaco Canyon: agriculture and location of, 12-13; architecture and interpretation of, 23-31; and Chaco phenomenon, 3; characteristics of in early period, 20-21; communities and Chaco world, 71-77; construction of in early twelfth century, 6; and domestic refuse, 15, 127; function of, 4-5; house mounds in San Juan Basin as precursors of, 18-20; and Mesa Verde region, 109-15; and new view of Chaco's origins, 21; and ritual centers, 103-104; and size of communities, 5; and socio-political organization, 95-97; stone masonry and architecture of, 16-18, *94, 125*; and turquoise artifacts, 38; visibility of and land scape, 80-82. *See also* architecture; Chetro Ketl; outliers; Peñasco Blanco; Pueblo Alto; Pueblo Bonito
great kivas: and astronomical alignments, 83; and Chaco phenomenon, 3; at Chetro Ketl, *51, 52*; and great houses, 82, 110; and pit houses, 15, 26; and turquoise artifacts, 38. *See also* kivas
Great Pueblo Architecture of Chaco Canyon (Lekson, 1984), 25
Greece, and religious centers, 104-105
Greenlee, Bill, *124*
Guadalupe Ruin, 73, *74*, 81
Guatemala, and transport of pottery, *39*

Hagstrom, Melissa, 128
Harrison, Gerald, *124*
Harrison, William H., 66
Hasch'éé Yá'li' (Navajo), 57
Hasuse, A., *124*
Hawley, Florence Ellis, 119
Hayes, Alden C., 24, 25, 29, 80, 121
herraduras (masonry enclosures), 76
Hewett, Edgar Lee, 7, 65-66, 119-20
Hisatsinom (Hopi), 41-47
history. *See* archaeology; Navajo; oral history and oral tradition
Hopi, and oral tradition on Chaco Canyon, 41-47. *See also* Pueblo
Hosta Butte, 83
household: and basic tool kit for daily use, 34; and pottery production, 128
Hovenweep National Monument, 89, 113
Huérfano Mountain, 16, 29, 80
Hyde, Frederick, 65, 66
Hyde Exploring Expedition, 65-66, *116*, 117, *126*
Hye, Thomas, 64

iconography, and Chaco Canyon as ritual center, 103
importation, of artifacts and food into Chaco Canyon,
    36-40, 127-28
interaction sphere, and Chaco Canyon, 73
irrigation systems, in Chaco Canyon: and agricultural
    patterns, 11, *12*; great houses and control of, 12-13;
    and sociopolitical complexity, 2. *See also* agriculture

Jackson, William Henry, 7
Jacobson, LouAnn, *124*
Jemez Mountains, 36
Judd, Neil M., 118, *119*
Judge, W. James, 121, *122*, *124*, 126, *129*

Kantner, John, 126, 127
katsina ceremonies, 41, 44
Keres, and oral tradition, 83
Kern brothers, 64
Kin Bineola, 21, 58, 81
Kin Kletso, 58, 91, 119, 120-21
Kin Kletso: A Pueblo III Community in Chaco Canyon
    (Vivian & Mathews), 24
Kin Klizhin, 81
Kin Nahasbas, 119
kinship, and sociopolitical organization of Chaco
    Canyon, 125, 127
Kintigh, Keith, 29
Kin'Ya'a Ruin, 56-57, 58, 74
kivas: and development of Chacoan great-house architec-
    ture, 26-27; and Hopi oral tradition, 47; and tur-
    quoise artifacts, 38. *See also* great kivas; tower kivas
Knapp, Bernard, 80
Kutz Canyon, 83

labor: and agriculture in Chaco Canyon, 11, 12; and
    construction of Chacoan great houses, 27
Lambert, Marjorie, 119
land-intensive systems, of agriculture, 11, 12
landscape: and astronomical alignments, 83-84; and built
    environment of Chaco Canyon, 28-29; and contem-
    porary Pueblo ideology, 79-80; and Navajo material
    culture, 58; and roads, 82-83; and time, 84-85; and
    visibility of great houses, 80-82. *See also* environment
land ownership, and history of Navajo in Chaco region,
    66, 67-69
leadership, and debate on sociopolitical organization of
    Chaco Canyon, 124-27
LeBlanc, Stephen, 128
Lekson, Stephen H., 10, 12, 25, 80, 83, 84, 123, *124*,
    126, 129

Leyit Kin, 119
line-of-sight system, and communication network, 29,
    82, 92
Lister, Florence, *121*
Lister, Robert H., 121, *122*
Lopez, Daniel, *124*
Lowry Ruin (Colorado), 111

macaws, 38-39
McElmo phase, and massing in Chacoan building, 28
McKenna, Peter, *124*
McPhee Pueblo, 16-17, *18*
maize, 37, 38, 107. *See also* agriculture
Malta, and prehistoric temples, 102, 103, *111*
Malville, J. McKim, 110
*Man Corn: Cannibalism and Violence in the American
    Southwest* (Turner & Turner, 1999), 112
Marshall, Michael, 80, 83
Martin, Paul, 111
Martinez, J., *124*
Masaw (Hopi), 41, 44, 45
massing, and construction of Chacoan great houses,
    27-28
material culture: of contemporary Navajo, 58; and ritual,
    103
Mathien, Joan, *129*
Matthews, Thomas, 23, 120
Maya, and calendars, 88
Mesa Verde National Park, 113
Mesa Verde region: and Chacoan great houses, 109-15;
    cultural history of, 107, 109; and oral traditions of
    Hopi, 44; and pit houses, 26. *See also* San Juan
    Basin
metates, 36, *37*
Meyer, Daniel, 126
migration: and depopulation of Mesa Verde region in late
    1200s, 111, 114-15; and oral traditions of Hopi,
    41-47; and reconstruction of pathways out of Chaco
    Canyon, 129-30. *See also* population
mining industry, 69
Mississipian sites, as ceremonial and political centers,
    30-31
Mockingbird Canyon, *11*
monumental tradition, and Chacoan architecture, 29-31,
    102-103
Morgan, Jacob C., 68
Morgan, Lewis Henry, 71
Morris, Earl H., 71
Motisinom (Hopi), 41, 42, 43
Museum of New Mexico, 23

house architecture, 25-26; as elite residence, 27; and history of archaeology in Chaco Canyon, 23, 117; and Hopi oral tradition, 41, 47; massing and building of, 27-28; McPhee Pueblo compared to, 17; and metates, *37*; and Navajo oral history, 58; and pottery, 98, *105*, *127*; reconstruction of, *96*; and turquoise artifacts, 37, 38; visibility of and landscape, 80

Pueblo I period: and adobe structure underlying Casa del Rio, 18; and cultural history of Mesa Verde region, 107, 115; and small houses in Chaco Canyon, 23, *24*; and stone masonry architecture of Chacoan great houses, 16

Pueblo II period, and San Juan River drainage, 115

Pueblo III period: and archaeological record for Mesa Verde region, 112, 113, 114; biological and cultural ancestry of modern Pueblo peoples and, 115

Pueblo Revolt (1680), 61

Quade, Jay, 128

rabbits, 37

railroads, and land ownership in Chaco region, 66, 67

Ratti, B., *124*

redistribution, and economies of religious and pilgrimage centers, 106

Red Mesa Valley, 35, 71, 80

Red Willow site, 84

refuse. See trash mounds

Reiter, Paul, 119

religion, and Navajo in Chaco region, 63. *See also* belief system; ceremony and ceremonial centers; pilgrimages; ritual

reservation, and Navajo, 66, 67

Rio Grande area, and migration from Mesa Verde region, 115

ritual: role of in Chacoan sociopolitical organization, 95, 97-98, 99, 126-27; system of in Chaco Canyon, 5; view of Chaco Canyon as center for, 101-106. *See also* belief system; ceremony and ceremonial centers; kivas; pilgrimages; religion

roads, *85, 102*: Casa del Rio as nexus of, 20; and Chaco phenomenon, 3; and great houses in San Juan Basin, 73, 75-76, 122; and landscape of Chaco Canyon, 82-83; as ritual pathways, 126; through time, 84

Roberts, Frank H. H., 71

rock art. *See* petroglyphs

Roll, S., 124

Roney, John, 75, 82

Roosevelt, Franklin D., 68

Roosevelt, Theodore, 66, 118

Sahara desert, and calendar circles, 87

Saint Michael's Mission, 66

Salapa site, 44

Salmon Ruin, 73, 109, *110*, 112, 113, 114

Sand Canyon Pueblo, 113

sand-dune dam, and water tables in Chaco Canyon, 2, 9, *10*, 12

Sandoval (Navajo), 64

San Juan Basin: aridity of environment in, 6, *34;* Chaco Canyon as architectural and ceremonial center of, 5; and early settlements in vicinity of Chaco Canyon, 16; and geographic centrality of Chaco Canyon, 82; and great houses outside Chaco Canyon, 72-73, 122; house mounds as precursors of Chacoan great houses, 18-20; map of, *xii*; and population increase prior to eleventh century, 2; reconstructions of climate in, 1. *See also* Mesa Verde region

Santa Clara Pueblo, 49-50

Santo Domingo Pueblo, *130*

Sargent, Edward, 65, 67

scheduling, of ceremonial events, 40. *See also* time

Schelberg, John, *124*

School of American Research, *52,* 118, *119*, *129*

Sebastian, Lynne, 126

settlement, Puebloan pattern of in Chaco Canyon, 15. *See also* migration; pit houses and pithouse villages; population; small houses and small-house sites

Shabik'eshchee Village, 15, 58

Shepard, Anna, 119

Simpson, Lt. James H., 64

small houses and small-house sites, *99*: and agriculture in Chaco Canyon, 11-12, 13; and architecture of Chacoan great houses, 25; and Pueblo I period, 23, *24*; and turquoise artifacts, 38

smallpox epidemic, and Navajo, 63

Smithsonian Institution, 23

social adaptation, to food shortages in Chaco Canyon, 11-13

social archaeology, 130

social relationships, and interpretation of artifacts, 33, 39-40

social status, and evidence for differentiation in Chaco Canyon, 95, 125

sociopolitical organization, and interpretations of Chaco Canyon, 1, 2, 93-99, 106, 124-27

"sodality," and explanations of Chaco phenomenon, 3

Sofaer, Anna, 28, 29, 83, 84

South Road, 75, 76, 81, 83, *84*

Southwest: and Chacoan architecture as unique, 30; great houses in northern, 73-74; role of Chaco in